THE ACID HOUSE

a screenplay by
Irvine Welsh

Methuen Film

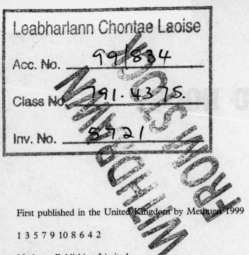

First published in the United Kingdom by Methuen 1999

1 3 5 7 9 10 8 6 4 2

Methuen Publishing Limited
20 Vauxhall Bridge Road, London SW1V 2SA

Random House Australia (Pty) Limited
20 Alfred Street, Milsons Point, Sydney, New South Wales 2061, Australia
Random House New Zealand Limited
18 Poland Road, Glenfield, Auckland 10, New Zealand
Random House South Africa (Pty) Limited
Endulini, 5A Jubilee Road, Parktown 2193, South Africa

Methuen Publishing Limited Reg. No. 3543167

A CIP catalogue record for this book is available from the British Library

ISBN 0 413 72420 4

Typeset by Deltatype Limited, Birkenhead, Merseyside
Printed and bound in Great Britain by Cox & Wyman Ltd, Reading, Berkshire

CONTENTS

INTRODUCTION

I wrote *The Acid House* (short stories) while the publishers were getting ready to put out *Trainspotting*. As a result, it only came out six months later; which is a very short time between new books. I thought, I'll fire it out before the inevitable backlash starts, which, as it happens, took a bit (but not that much) longer than I thought.

I had another book (unpublished) ready, which was basically a continuation of *Trainspotting*. However, I was sick of the characters by that time and decided that I wanted to write something fresh, so I started writing short stories. In fact, I never really stopped, as *Trainspotting* and it's unpublished follow-up are more of a series of stories than a novel. So I soon had enough for *The Acid House*. Ironically, *The Acid House* was the more popular book of the two in the first year of publication. *Trainspotting* had brilliant reviews, many calling it a modern classic, but in it's first year it sold practically fuck all. It was only when clubby types started buying *The Acid House*, then backtracked into *Trainspotting*, that it started to shift from shelves. That was when I lost interest in critics; once you find your readership you have that luxury. Good reviews are a solace if you don't sell; hostile reviews are an optional tax if you do. I was never too keen on paying optional taxes.

Then came the play and the film of *Trainspotting*, which took it to new commercial heights, both here and abroad. That was good for me as it made me enough money not to give a toss, thankfully, before I'd even had time to learn to do so. I had no involvement with writing the stage or screenplays of *Trainspotting*, except to offer words of support/advice/encouragement to Harry Gibson (play) and John Hodge (film), which, to be frank, neither of them really needed. At that point I didn't really fancy doing any stage or screenwriting; basically because I had just packed in the day job, had moved to Amsterdam, finished the *Marabou Stork Nightmares* and was trying to get used to the idea of lounging around in hash bars doing nothing. To my surprise, it was quite easy. However, I was torn from this semi-contented slumber by Alex Usborne, David Muir and Carolynne Sinclair. They wanted me to adapt some of my stories in *The Acid House* for the screen.

My attitude to writing is, fuck it, I'll have a go. I didn't expect to write a book in the first place, let alone get it published. That's probably the most difficult thing in writing over and done with, so anything else is just Green Shield Stamps or Embassy Regal coupons: collect the set and get an alarm clock and lung cancer. So I never wanted to be too precious about the medium I wrote in, whether it was a novel, short story, stage or screenplay, a poem or a song. It's just something that you get on with.

Speaking practically though, *The Acid House* was a good place for me to start screenwriting; the small digestable chunks that are stories, rather than the scripting of one of my larger pieces of fiction, or, more daunting, the writing of a complete original screenplay. *The Acid House* was originally conceived as a series of short films for Channel Four. I would script from one to three stories from the book which would be shown on television.

I previously had a small go at screenwriting, for the Tartan Shorts series. What I produced was basically shite, and the telly people were wise rejecting it out of hand. It was fruitful for me though, as through this venture I met Carolynne Sinclair who put me in touch with Stuart Cosgrove at

Channel Four. We then got hooked up with David Muir at Umbrella Productions and Alex Usborne at Picture Palace North in Sheffield. Alex had been interested in us doing something together for a while and had sent me his *Tales From a Hard City*, which I had enjoyed. They wanted to co-produce television films from *The Acid House*. The idea was that they would have a different director for each one. As is often the way with those things, the dosh came in different bundles, so we shot the first one, *The Granton Star Cause*, far in advance of the next two, with Paul McGuigan directing.

In the meantime, *Trainspotting*, the film of my first novel, had proved to be a great cinematic success. I'm not boasting – there's no other way I can put it. This obviously led the parties involved, including me, to conclude that *The Acid House* had large screen potential. Let's be blunt: you get far more money and kudos from a big-screen film than you do from a TV film, and, crucially, you don't have to put up with nearly as many whinging fuckers telling you that it's disgusting and obscene etc etc, because you're not 'invading' their living rooms. (Top tip: there's a marvellous invention called the on-off switch and an interesting concept called 'freedom of choice'; I find that a combination of the two invariably produces satisfying viewing.)

Anyway, I finished the subsequent adaptations of the stories, *A Soft Touch* and *The Acid House*. Everybody was very keen to have Paul direct the other two, so as to have some sort of continuity of style, but more importantly, because we were highly delighted with the work he'd done on *The Granton Star Cause*. When I got hooked up with Danny Boyle for *Trainspotting* and saw the final result, I thought, 'fuck me, I've done alright here'. After seeing Paul's offering, I got exactly the same vibe. It was a bit like winning the lottery twice in a row.

The Granton Star Cause was shown on TV as a pilot for the entire film. In the event of this, a slightly different and sharper edit appears on the big-screen version. There was a supposed 'controversy' about the TV screening. They're funny things, controversies. In this case it meant that some bored sub-editor on a right-wing newspaper read by a few sad cunts decided to delve into their box-file of rent-a-quote cranks and run the contents of the film past them. They got a few self-righteous publicity seekers to foam at the mouth in print for their readers, then the other 'intelligent' sections of the press and broadcasting media slavishly picked it up. I was invited on to a discussion programme, chaired by Pat Kane, to discuss the controversy. As there wasn't one to discuss I saw no point in going along. Obviously Kevin Williamson hadn't bothered to put his name up for the pool so he went along to listen to a Daily Express hack say how crap and disgusting it was, only for a deluge of real people to phone in and say it was cool. But controversy? My arse.

Prior to this, at the Edinburgh Film Festival, Andy O'Hagan had chaired a panel which included some churchy types and the actor Maurice Roeves who played God in the film. Once again I was invited, but declined to appear. I think it may have clashed with a third division match on Sky or something. Controversial? Not as far as I'm concerned.

Anyway, we shot the other two, which were even better than the first one. Nice one, or rather, nice three, Paul. On a personal level, I was delighted with *A Soft Touch* as Gary McCormack, who is electrifying as Larry, is an all-drinking, all-clubbing, Hibees buddy-about-town of mine. He cornered me in the bogs at The Pure some years back, and told me that he wanted me to get him an audition for *Trainspotting*. Gary had never acted before. A lot of pals were coming up to me when they were off their tits and asking me to get them auditions, only to forget all about it the next day. I should have known with Gary, though, that it would run a wee bit deeper than that. However, I'm ashamed to say that when I moved to Amsterdam I forgot all about Gaz's request. The film was shot and the rest is known.

x

The next time I was out clubbing with Gary he shot me that wounded stag look and reminded me that I'd forgotten to make that phone call to Danny Boyle and Andrew McDonald about an audition. Fortunately, I was able to make amends, and Paul, Alex, David and Carolynne agreed to see him. Gary, in the meantime, had learned the entire script, not just his own lines, and blew everybody away at the audition, then on the set. *Star* had already been cast; he did a small part in it, but then he emerged as Larry in *A Soft Touch*. That *ménage à trois* of Larry, Catriona (Michelle Gomez) and Johnny (Kevin McKidd) works brilliantly on the screen. I knew Michelle from one of the versions of the *Trainspotting* play and from *Headstate*, and she brings that awesome power to the screen as much as she does to the stage. While Gary and Michelle are amazing as the bad bastards, and Ewan Bremner, Steven McCole and Maurice Roeves turn in great performances; the real star acting performance in my book comes from Kevin McKidd as Johnny. An actor of lesser ability would have been swamped, surrounded by Larry, Catriona and Tam Dean Burn's Alec all going berserk around him, but Kevin held the whole thing together with a performance of incredible empathy, sensitivity and control. *A Soft Touch* is probably my favourite of the trio, it's the most hardcore and unsentimental; I like to see great acting performances in the cinema and I think it's the best thing I've seen in that direction since Ray Winstone and Kathy Burke out Di Niro'ed Di Niro in *Nil By Mouth*.

The Acid House is a thundering trip of a short film in which visuals and music are used to great effect to tell the interwoven stories of Coco and baby Tom. Ewan Bremner is at his expressive best in it. I know Ewan from both the stage and screen versions of *Trainspotting* and I think he's one of the most gifted actors around. It was great to have Jemma Redgrave and Martin Clunes involved, especially as you wouldn't associate them with my stuff. It was flattering for me that they both showed an interest, not just because they are huge television stars (they certainly weren't doing it for money, no danger, eh Alex, David?), but because they're both enormous talents. So hopefully, as they say, there's something for all the family. It starts on a high, gets nasty and ends on a high.

When I saw the three films put together for the first time, I was delighted. I think that it isn't going to be as commercially successful as *Trainspotting*, as we decided, fairly early on, to take a different approach and not air-brush it for the mass-market. A lot of the more sheepish elements, who felt the need to jump on the *Trainspotting* bandwagon, might find some of it a wee bit hard to take, but hopefully the punters who were into the books right from the start; the wideo's, the cognoscenti, the Hibs boys and girls, the clubbers and the rest of the motley crew will love it.

This one's for them.

Irvine Welsh
June 1998

THE ACID HOUSE

THE GRANTON STAR CAUSE

INT. CHANGING ROOMS. EARLY AFTERNOON.

The players and officials of Granton Star F.C. are in the changing rooms preparing for a match. The principal characters are BOAB COYLE, KEVIN *(who is team Captain),* GRANT *and* TAMBO. *They are in their strips and lacing up their boots. The* PARKIE *is sweeping up around them. His cassette player is loudly playing 'Supersonic' by Oasis and he is singing along enthusiastically to it.*

KEV (*stage loudly towards the Parkie*): Ah just hope these fuckin showers are workin this time.

BOAB: Doesnae bother me if they arenae. Ah'm no wantin tae go in the showers wi you anywey. Might catch something.

GRANT: Tell ye what Boab, we'll pit ye in the showers wi that wee winger fae thair team. Thir's nae chance ay you catchin anything fae him. Ye nivir goat near um the last time!

BOAB: Ah'll sort him oot this time!

KEV: Make sure ye do Boab. Hit um. Hit um hard. That's the only wey yi'll stoap that nippy wee cunt.

BOAB: It's only a fuckin game . . . ah dinnae want tae brek the wee guy's leg . . .

KEV (*up close to* BOAB): Hit um fuckin hard Boab. Thir no makin cunts oot ay us. Right!

BOAB: Right . . .

The players exit. The PARKIE *watches them go.*

PARKIE: Fuck!

EXT. FOOTBALL PITCH. MID-AFTERNOON.

We see scenes from the game in progress; a goal from TAMBO, BOAB *being mutmegged by a nippy wee winger which leads to equaliser. . . .*

TITLES:

THE GRANTON STAR CAUSE

. . . KEV *scoring the winner.*

INT. PUBLIC HOUSE. LATE AFTERNOON.

A gang of players from the local Churches League football team come in and head up to the bar. We focus particularly on three; KEVIN, GRANT *and* TAMBO. *The players are very animated and excited.*

BARMAN (*to team skipper, who is smiling broadly*): How did it go Kev?

KEV: Nicked it Pat; two—one. Yours truly playing the captain's part and knockin hame the winner. We wir a bit scabby if the truth be telt, but these mugs never made the best ay the possession. Ye kin huv aw the possession in the world but if ye cannae make it count . . .

RONNIE: Good stuff. That's a wee run now, eh.

KEV: Aye, wir hopin fir promotion and gaun aw the wey in the Tom Logan memorial trophy. Jist tae git the fill treatment at City Park, wi the nets n aw that stuff. The real game, ye ken? Ah mean these cunts were disputing our first goal the day . . .

GRANT: Aye, it's no the same withoot the nets . . . eh, three pints Pat.

TAMBO: The baw has tae hit the back ay the net. That's the essence ay the game. That's when ye ken yir playin real fitba n no jist huvin a kick aboot . . . eh, just a fresh orange n lemonade for me Pat. Goat the car likes, ken.

KEV: Of course Pat, we have tae effect the necessary personnel changes tae ensure we continue tae make the progress required by Granton Star Football Club F.C.

TAMBO: You gaunny tell Boab Coyle he's droaped then?

KEV: Look, ah sais ah would. Ah'm the captain, ah'll tell um: mates or nae mates. The Granton Star cause has tae come first. Boab'll understand, eh.

GRANT: Aye, right!

The passage of time is indicated by the clock and the increased inebriation of the players. BOAB *is at the other end of the bar, unaware of the conversation his friends are quietly having. The clock behind the bar now reads 7:45.*

GRANT: If ye dinnae tell um now Kev, ye never will.

KEV: Ah'll tell um.

TAMBO: Look, if ye'd rather somebody else brought it up, wi n him bein good mates likes . . .

KEV: Look, ah telt ye Tambo, ah'll bring it up.

TAMBO: When?

KEV: Right! Ah'll fuckin well dae it now!

KEV *moves over to* BOAB. *He leads him by the arm along to a quieter spot at the bar.*

KEV: Look Boab, ah've goat something tae tell ye mate.

BOAB: What's that then? Aboot Wednesday night? We'll take five oaf the cunts! Let me play further forward this time though Kev. Ah might no huv the pace, but ah could spray it aboot a bit, ken what a mean?

KEV: Listen mate, this isnae easy tae say. It's jist thit we aw agree; we cannae guarantee ye a game any mair.

BOAB: Eh . . .

KEV: Ye see, it's aw aboot depth ay pool Boab. We've goat Tambo and wee Grant now. This team's gaun places.

BOAB: Gaun places!? Gaun places!? Churches League Division Three! It's a kick aboot, ya pretentious cunt!

A fuckin kick aboot!

KEV: Yir bound tae be disappointed mate . . .

BOAB: Disappointed!? Too fuckin right ah'm disappointed.
Which cunt washes the strips nearly every week? Eh?

KEV: C'moan mate, huv another pint . . .

BOAB: Stick yir fuckin pint up yir erse! Some mates yous,
eh? Well fuck yis!

BOAB *storms out of the pub.*

EXT. STREET IN A COUNCIL SCHEME. EARLY EVENING.

BOAB *walks down the street, which is like West Granton Road
or some other main road, towards his parents' house. It is
located in a standard Edinburgh post-war tenement block, six
houses in the stair. The bottom ones with the gardens may
have been bought. The block has a satellite dish on the side of
it.* BOAB *is talking to himself and kicking a can violently.*

BOAB: That orange juice drinking wee poof Tambo . . .
he's only just fuckin joined the club . . .

BOAB *puts on a high, nasal whine:*

. . . fresh orange n lemonade . . . fresh orange n
lemonade . . .

. . . well ah'll show these cunts . . . ah'll git another
fuckin club, nae fuckin bother at aw . . .

*He heads into a stair, within which is the home of his
parents,* DOREEN *and* BOAB SENIOR.

INT. COUNCIL HOUSE. EARLY EVENING.

BOAB *and* DOREEN *are in the front room of their home
watching television. The house is a shrine to the seventies, with
an abundance of teak and a sunhouse electric fire. The
television and video equipment is state-of-the-art though, the*

8

monitor has a large, flat screen. A new video camera is
connected up to it on a tripod.

DOREEN: That'll be him now, Boab.

BOAB SENIOR: Aye, Doe, ah'll tell um.

As BOAB *enters, his father casts his newspaper on the*
table and gives his mother a brief conspiratorial nod.

BOAB SENIOR: Awright son? Ah want a wee word wi ye.

BOAB: Aw aye?

DOREEN: S'no likesay we're tryin tae git rid ay ye, son.
S'no likesay that at aw.

BOAB SENIOR (*to* DOREEN): That's enough, Doreen. Lit
me speak tae the laddie.

BOAB: What's aw this aboot?

BOAB SENIOR: The thing is, son, it's time you were oot ay
this hoose. Yir twenty-three years auld now, which is
far too auld fir a laddie tae be steyin wi his ma n
faither. Ah mean, ah wis away tae sea wi the
Merchant Navy at seventeen . . . It's jist no natural,
son, d'ye understand?

Ah mean, ye dinnae want yir mates tae think thit yir
some kind ay queer felly, now dae ye? Anywey, me n
yir ma's no gittin any younger. Wir enterin a funny
phase in oor lives, son; some might say . . . a
dangerous phase. Yir ma n me son, we need time tae
sort oot our lives. Tae git it the gither, if ye ken what
ah mean. You've goat a lassie, wee Evelyn. You ken
the score!

Yir problem is, son . . .

BOAB: Naw bit . . .

BOAB SENIOR: Hear ays oot son . . .

DOREEN (*to* BOAB SENIOR): It wisnae meant tae be like
this Boab.

BOAB SENIOR: It's no like anything though, Doreen. Thir's
nae hassle: jist a faither-tae-son talk. Aw ah'm sayin
tae the laddie, aw ah'm sayin tae ye, Boab, is thit yir

9

huvin yir cake n eatin it. N whae suffers? Ah'll tell ye whae: muggins here. Yir ma n me. Now ah ken that it's no that easy tae find somewhair tae stey these days, especially when yuv hud somebody else, like muggins here, runnin aroond eftir ye. Bit we'll no say nowt aboot that the now. Thing is, me n yir ma, wir prepared tae gie ye two weeks' grace. Jist as long as yir oot ay here within a fortnight.

BOAB: Aye . . . right . . .

DOREEN: Dinnae think thit wir tryin tae git rid ay ye, son, it's jist thit yir faither n me think thit it wid be mutually advantageous tae baith parties, likesay, if ye found yir ain place.

BOAB SENIOR: That's it, Doe! Mutually advantageous tae baith parties. Ah like that! Any brains you n oor Cathy've goat, son, they came fae yir ma thair, nivir mind muggins here.

BOAB: Right.

BOAB *is dejected and turns to leave.*

DOREEN: Dinnae jist rush oot again though, son. Sit doon n watch bit ay the telly.

BOAB SENIOR: Doe! Lit the laddie go oot! He'll want tae be oot wi his mates or wee Evelyn. He'll no want tae sit here watchin the telly wi us! We're . . . jist, eh . . . huvin a play wi the new toy, son.

BOAB SENIOR *gestures at the video camera. A lecherous glance flits between him and his wife which* BOAB *does not quite understand but which still makes him uneasy.*

BOAB: Aye . . . see yis.

BOAB *leaves the flat.*

EXT. STREET. EVENING.

BOAB *walks down the street.*

BOAB (*to himself*): Evelyn . . . Evelyn . . . thank fuck for you, hen . . . Evelyn . . . mibbee we should git a place the gither. Ev'll be intae that! That's the one! Watch what ah want tae watch oan the telly. A ride every night. Wake up tae a blow-job every morning. Git the strips washed whin ah git another club! (*Sings.*) Here we go, here we go, here we go!

INT. PHONE-BOX. EVENING.

BOAB *enters the phone-box and dials* EVELYN's *number. It connects. As they talk we cut between them.* EVELYN *is in her room which has a poster of Jarvis Cocker from Pulp and Darren Jackson of Hibs F.C. on the wall. She is idly making up her eyes.*

BOAB: Ev? Boab. Awright?

EVELYN: Aye.

BOAB: Fancy comin' ower? (EVELYN *lets the silence hang.*) Eh? Ev? Fancy comin ower, likesay?

EVELYN: Naw.

BOAB: How no?

EVELYN: Jist dinnae.

BOAB: Bit how no?

EVELYN: Jist dinnae.

BOAB: Bit how no? Ah've hud a bad day, Ev. Ah need tae talk tae ye.

EVELYN: Aye. Well, talk tae yir mates well.

BOAB: Dinnae be like that, Ev! Ah sais ah've hud a hard day! Whit is it? Whit huv ah done?

EVELYN: You ken.

BOAB: Ev . . .

EVELYN: It's no what yuv done, it's what yuv no done!

BOAB: But, Ev . . .

EVELYN: Me n you, Boab. Ah want a guy whae kin dae

11

things fir ays. Somebody whae kin really make love tae a woman. No just some fat bastard whae sits oan his erse talkin aboot the fitba n drinkin pints ay lager wi his mates. A real man, Boab, a sexy man. Ah'm twinty, Boab, twinty years auld. Ah'm no gaunny tie masel doon tae a slob!

BOAB: What's goat into you? Eh? Evelyn? Ye nivir complained before. You n me. You wir jist a daft wee lassie before ye met me. Nivir knew whit a ride wis, fir fuck sake . . .

EVELYN: Aye! Well that's aw changed! Cos ah've met somebody, Boab Coyle! Mair ay a fuckin man thin you'll ivir be!

BOAB: Eh? . . . Eh? . . . Whae!?! . . . Whae is the cuuuuhhhnnnt!!???

EVELYN: That's fir me tae ken n you tae find oot.

BOAB: Bit, Ev . . . how could you dae this tae ays . . . you n me, Ev . . . it wis eywis you n me . . . engagement n that . . .

EVELYN: Sorry, Boab. Bit ah've been wi you ever since ah wis sixteen. Ah might huv kent nowt aboot love then, but ah sure as fuck ken a bit mair now.

BOAB: Ya faahkin slag! . . . Ya horrible fuckin hing-oot!

EVELYN: That's us finished, Boab.

BOAB: What ur ye sayin?

EVELYN: Wir finished. Finito. Kaput. Endy story. Goodnight Vienna.

EVELYN *slams the receiver down.*

BOAB (*to receiver and dead line*): Ev . . . Ev . . . ah love ye . . . (BOAB *freaks out and starts booting out the glass panels of the phone-box, unaware that a police car has pulled up alongside him.*) Slaahht! Faahkin slaaahhht! BOAB *looks up to be confronted by the police officers and is taken into the car.*

12

INT. POLICE STATION. EVENING.

A sergeant, MORRISON, *is being escorted around the cells by*
P.C. COCHRANE.

P.C. COCHRANE: Sarge.

SERGEANT MORRISON: Brian. So, what's all been
happening tonight?

P.C. COCHRANE: Well, there's the rapist, the boy that
stabbed the guy at the shopping centre and this
comedian here.

SERGEANT MORRISON: Right . . . well, ah've been doon
and hud a word wi the rapist already. Seems a nice
enough young felly. Telt ays that the hoor wis asking
for it. S'the wey ay the world, Brian. The guy who
knifed the boy, well, silly bugger, but boys will boys.
(MORRISON *looks at* BOAB *with great distaste.*) What
aboot this tube-stake?

P.C. COCHRANE: Caught him smashin up a phone-box.
SERGEANT MORRISON *clenches his teeth shut. He is
trying to contain a surge of anger which threatens to
overwhelm him.*

SERGEANT MORRISON: Ah want a wee word wi this cunt.

INT. CELLS IN BASEMENT OF POLICE STATION. EVENING.
SERGEANT MORRISON *has* BOAB *at his mercy and applies a
policeman's professional kicking to his prisoner, hitting him
where the marks are least likely to show. As a beaten-up* BOAB
lies at his feet, MORRISON *addresses him on his political
philosophy.*

SERGEANT MORRISON: Ye ken, it jist goes tae show ye the
effectiveness ay they privatisation policies. Ah wid
nivir have reacted like that if ye had smashed one up
when they were nationalised. The thing is though, son,

13

as a BT shareholder, I feel as if ah've got mair ay a
stake now, and I dinnae want any lumpen-proletarian
malcontent threatening my investment.

INT. LOADING BAY OF A DEPOT. MORNING.
Two men in overalls, BENNY *and* ZIPPO, *are with* BOAB
loading furniture on and off a series of vans and lorries.

ZIPPO: Michael O'Neill ghosts it fae the left n hits it
    square tae Jackson. He lets it run, and thairs Harper,
    blastin it past the Motherwell goalie. Ye should've
    been thair, man.
BENNY: Ah hud that fuckin weddin.
BOAB: Ah would've went, but we hud a game oan. Won
    two–one. Ah wis playin full-back. Ah wis up against it
    wi this winger. Good wee player. The speed ay this
    boy!
    DREW, *one of the workmates, approaches* BOAB.
DREW: Boab, the gaffer wants a word.
BOAB: Rafferty?
DREW: Aye.
BOAB: Did eh say what it wis aboot?
DREW: Like fuck. That cunt's no likely tae tell the likes ay
    me fuck all, now, is eh?
BOAB: Aye, right enough.
    BOAB *heads towards* RAFFERTY's *office as* BENNY,
    DREW *and* ZIPPO *look sombrely at each other.*

INT. OFFICE IN DEPOT. MORNING.
The gaffer, MIKE RAFFERTY, *is sitting in his small office,
which is just a wood and glass box in the corner of the depot,
when* BOAB *comes in.*

14

RAFFERTY: Sit doon, Boab. I'll come right tae the point, mate.

BOAB: Aye . . .

RAFFERTY: Standards. (RAFFERTY *points to a large plaque behind him. It bears the logo of the Hauliers and Removals Association, a logo which decorates every one of his fleet of lorries.*) Counts for nothing now. It's aw about price these days, Boab. And all these cowboys, who have fewer overheads and lower costs, they're trimming us, Boab.

BOAB: Whir ur ye tryin tae say?

RAFFERTY: We've goat tae cut costs, Boab. Where can ah cut costs? This place? No. It has to be capital and labour costs. It's aw doon tae market positioning, Boab. We have to find our niche in the market. That niche is as a quality firm specialising in local moves for the As, Bs and Cs.

BOAB: So ah'm sacked?

RAFFERTY: Your post is being made redundant, Boab. It's important to remember that it's not the person we make redundant, it's the post. We've overstretched ourselves, Boab. Got geared up for continental removals. Tried, and I have to say failed, to compete with the big boys. Got a wee bit carried away by all this bullshit about the single market and all that crap. I'm going to have to let the big lorry go. We also need to lose a driver's job. This isnae easy, Boab, but it has to be the last one in, the first one out. Now ah'll put it around in the trade that I know of a reliable driver who's looking for something, and obviously, ah'll give you excellent references.

BOAB: Obviously.

BOAB *gets up and leaves.* RAFFERTY *starts to speak, but thinks better of it and lets him depart.* BOAB *leaves the depot, unnoticed by his workmates, and heads for a local pub.*

15

INT. PUBLIC HOUSE. LUNCHTIME.

BOAB *gets a pint and a toastie and sits down. Although the pub is empty, he is joined at his table by a man who looks in his late fifties, and has white hair and a beard, like a Celtic folk singer.*

MAN (to BOAB): Yuv fucked this one up, ya daft cunt.

BOAB: Eh? What?

MAN: You. Boab Coyle. Nae hoose, nae job, nae burd, nae mates, polis record, sair face, aw in the space ay a few ooirs. Nice one!

BOAB: How the fuck dae you ken ma business! What's it goat tae do wi you!

MAN: It's ma fuckin business tae ken! Ah'm God!

BOAB: Way tae fuck ya auld radge!

GOD: Fuckin hell; another wise cunt. Robert Anthony Coyle, born on Friday the 23rd of July to Robert McNamara Coyle and Doreen Sharp. Younger brother of Cathleen Siobhain Shaw, who is married to James Allan Shaw. They live at 21 Parkglen Crescent in Gilmerton and they have a child, also called James. You have a sickle-shaped birthmark on your inner thigh. You attended Granton Primary School and Ainslie Park Secondary, where you obtained two SCE O Grades, in Woodwork and Technical Drawing. Until recently, you worked in furniture removals, lived at hame, hud a bird called Evelyn, whom you couldn't sexually satisfy, and played football for Granton Star, like you made love, employing little effort and even less skill.

BOAB: If you're God, what ur ye daein wastin time oan the likes ay me?

GOD: Good question, Boab, good question.

16

BOAB: Ah mean, thir's bairns starvin, likesay, oan the telly
n that. If ye wir that good, ye could sort aw that
oot instead ay sitting here bevvyin wi the likes ay
me.

GOD: Hud oan a minute, pal. Lit's git one thing straight.
Every fuckin time ah come doon here, some wide-o
pills ays up aboot what ah should n shouldnae be
fuckin daein. Either that or ah huv tae enter intae
some philosophical discourse wi some wee
undergraduate twat aboot the nature ay masel, the
extent ay ma omnipotence n aw that shite. Ah'm gittin
a wee bit fed up wi aw this self-justification; it's no for
yous cunts tae criticise me. Ah made yous cunts in ma
ain image. Yous git oan wit it. Yous fuckin well sort it
oot. That cunt Nietzsche wis wide ay the mark when
eh sais thit ah wis deid. Ah'm no deid; ah jist dinnae
gie a fuck. Nae other cunt gies a fuck, so how should
ah? It's no fir me tae sort every cunt's problems oot.

BOAB: How's it no! You're a fuckin toss! See if ah hud
your fuckin powers . . .

GOD: If you hud ma powers ye'd dae what ye dae right
now: sweet fuck all. You've goat the power tae cut
doon oan the pints ay lager, aye?

BOAB: Aye, bit . . .

GOD: Nae buts aboot it. You've goat the power tae git fit
n make a mair positive contribution tae the Granton
Star cause. Ye hud the power tae pey mair attention
tae that wee burd ay yours. She wis tidy. Ye could've
done a loat better there Boab.

BOAB: Mibbe a could, mibbe ah couldnae. Whit's it tae
you?

GOD: Ye hud the power tae git oot fae under yir ma n
dad's feet so's they could huv a decent cowp in peace.
Bit naw. No selfish cunt Coyle. Jist sits thair watchin

Coronation Street n *Brookside* while they perr cunts ur
gaun up the waws wi frustration.

BOAB: S'nane ay your business!

GOD: Everything's ma business. Ye hud the power tae fight
back against that fat cunt fi the cafe. Ye jist lit the
cunt panel ye, fir a few fuckin pence. That wis oot ay
order, bit ye lit the cunt git away wi it.

BOAB: Ah wis in a state ay shock . . .

GOD: And that cunt Rafferty. Ye didnae even tell the cunt
tae stick his fuckin joab up his erse.

BOAB: So what! So fuckin what!

GOD: So ye hud they powers, ye jist couldnae be bothered
usin thum. That's why ah'm interested in ye Boab.
You're jist like me: a lazy apathetic, slovenly cunt.
Now ah hate bein like this, n bein immortal, ah
cannae punish masel. Ah kin punish you though,
mate. That's jist whit ah intend tae dae.

BOAB: But ah could . . .

GOD: Shut it cunt! Ah've fuckin hud it up tae ma eyebaws
wi aw this repentence shite. Vengeance is mine, n ah
intend tae take it, oan ma ain lazy n selfish nature,
through the species ah created, through thir
representative. That's you.

GOD *stands up.* BOAB *is scared and is trying to buy
time.*

BOAB: Ye look jist like ah always imagined . . .

GOD: That's cause ye've nae imagination, ya daft cunt. Ye
see ays n hear ays as ye imagine ays. Now you're
fuckin claimed, radge.

BOAB: But ah'm no the worst . . . whit aboot the
murderers, the serial killers, dictators, torturers,
politicians . . . the cunts thit shut doon factories tae
preserve thir profit levels . . . aw they greedy rich
bastards . . . what aboot thaim? Eh?

18

GOD: Might git roon tae they cunts, might no. That's ma
     fuckin business. You've hud it cunt! Yir a piece ay
     slime, Coyle. An insect. That's it! An insect! Ah'm
     gaunny make ye look like the dirty, lazy pest thit ye
     are! (GOD *looks* BOAB *in the eye, and projects a force of*
     energy out at him which pins him back in his chair. It's
     over in seconds, and BOAB *is shaken but unharmed. The*
     whole thing seems to have taken more out of GOD *who*
     staggers away from the table.) Ah'm away hame tae ma
     kip . . . (GOD *departs wheezing. He is hitting the side of*
     his head as he exits from the pub.) Some fucking day
     this . . .

     BOAB *sits in silence, trying to make sense of what has*
     happened to him. His friend KEVIN, *who dropped him*
     from Granton Star F.C. comes into the pub, but is
     reluctant to approach BOAB *at first. After a while he*
     comes over to join his friend.

KEV: Boab.

BOAB: Kev.

KEV: Look, Boab . . . sorry aboot the other day . . .

BOAB: Ah dinnae gie a fuck aboot the other day, aboot
      fitba, or aboot the Star. Ah've hud a fuckin bad time,
      Kev, n now ah've jist met God. The cunt's gaunny
      turn ays intae an insect.

KEV: Aye, right. Ah suppose it wid be easier thin turnin ye
     intae a fitba player, eh!

BOAB: Ah'm no fuckin jokin . . .

KEV: Ye dinnae half talk some shite, Boab.

INT. KEV'S HOUSE. EVENING.

KEV *is annoyed to notice a large* BLUEBOTTLE *on the edge of*
his plate. The BLUEBOTTLE *crawls into a blob of tomato*
sauce and flies up onto the wall. It starts to trace out KEV *on*

19

the white woodchip paper. KEV *is astonished.*) Boab? Is that really you? Fuckin hell! Eh, buzz twice fir aye, once fir naw.

BLUEBOTTLE: Buzz. Buzz.

KEV: Did, eh . . . what's his name, did eh, God dae this tae ye?

BLUEBOTTLE: Buzz. Buzz.

KEV: Whit the fuck ye gaunny dae? (*The* BLUEBOTTLE *buzzes frantically.*) Sorry Boab . . . kin ah git ye anything? Scran, likesay? (KEV *and the* BLUEBOTTLE *share the food on his plate.*) Yir welcome tae stay here, Boab. Jist keep oot ay Julie's wey, cause she hates flies. Stey behind the curtains in the spare room, right?

BLUEBOTTLE: Buzz. Buzz.

KEV: N nae sneakin in tae spy oan us while wir oan the job, ya dirty cunt, right?

BLUEBOTTLE: Buzz.

KEV: Does that mean naw ah will, or naw ah winnae? Buzz twice fir naw ah willnae sneak in tae watch Kev n Julie shaggin.

BLUEBOTTLE: Buzz. Buzz.

KEV: Good . . . want ays tae brek a bit mair fish oaf?

BLUEBOTTLE: Buzz. Buzz.

We see the BLUEBOTTLE *flying out of the window at* KEV*'s.*

EXT. SKY/TOWNSCAPE. MORNING.
BOAB *is soaring around over Granton. He is exhilarated by the power of flight.*

EXT. STREET. MORNING.

BOAB *as a fly, lands on a piece of hot shite which is crowded with several other flies. His long tongue is slurping happily at the faeces and he gives one of the sexy girl flies a saucy wink.*

INT. BEDROOM IN HOUSE. EVENING.

EVELYN, BOAB's *ex-girlfriend, and* TAMBO, *who replaced him in the Granton Star line-up, are shagging in the wreckage of a bedroom. They are going for it in a big way,* EVELYN *on top of him.*

TAMBO: Ooohhh . . . ooohhh . . . fuc-kin-hell . . .

EVELYN: . . . this is fuckin magic . . . ah love a good fuck . . . oohhh . . . oohh . . . the poppers . . .
  BOAB *the bluebottle buzzing at the window, watching* TAMBO *and* EVELYN *shagging.*

TAMBO: . . . aye . . . ah'm ready in aw, Ev . . . quick . . .
  EVELYN *reaches over and grabs two small bottles.*
  TAMBO *takes one. They break open the poppers and apply them to each other's nostrils as they climax.*

EVELYN: Oh Tambo . . . oohh . . . keep fucking me, Tambo . . .

TAMBO: . . . eh . . . it's you thit's fuckin me . . . fuck . . . fuugghhckkk . . .
  TAMBO *and* EVELYN *come together.*
  BLUEBOTTLE *slips into the house.*

INT. KITCHEN. EVENING.

BOAB *the bluebottle is standing on the side of a pot of curry, eating some of it and puking it back into the pot. He flies to the roof as* TAMBO *enters in his dressing gown and ignites the stove under it.*

TAMBO (*to himself*): That lassie isnae fuckin real. (*He grabs his crotch lightly.*) Mister Fuckin Rid-Raw Baws here.

INT. BATHROOM. EVENING.

TAMBO *and* EVELYN *are at the sink and bog-pan respectively, throwing up and groaning.*

INT. RAFFERTY'S OFFICE. DAYTIME.

RAFFERTY *is eating his sandwich at his desk. He is also on the phone.*

RAFFERTY: They should be there within the hour, Mrs
  Munro. Wait till I check the schedule . . .
  RAFFERTY *stands up, and goes into a filing cabinet. We pan to a bluebottle on a matchbox of rat poison. Then we pan over to the bluebottle which is crawling all over* RAFFERTY's *sandwich.*

EXT. OUTSIDE DEPOT. LATE AFTERNOON.

RAFFERTY *is being taken away in an ambulance. We see this from the view of* BOAB *as a fly.*

INT. FRONT ROOM OF BOAB'S PARENTS' HOUSE. EVENING.

BLUEBOTTLE *comes in through open window and flies onto the wall. Through the bluebottle's eyes we witness* BOAB's FATHER *clad in a black, nylon body-stocking with a hole at the crotch. His arms are outstretched with his hands on the mantelpiece and his legs apart.* BOAB's MOTHER *is naked apart from a belt, attached to which is a huge dildo, most of which but not all, is up* BOAB SENIOR's *arse. His father's head is hitting against a picture over the mantelpiece, which is of the 1972 Hibs League Cup winning side.*

22

BOAB SENIOR: Keep pushing, Doe . . . keep pushin . . . ah kin take mair . . . ah need mair . . . Herriot . . . Brownlie . . . Schaedler . . .

DOREEN: Wir nearly up tae the hilt already . . . yir an awfay man, Boab Coyle . . .

DOREEN continues to push the dildo.

BOAB SENIOR: . . . Stanton . . . Black . . . Blackley . . . the questionin, Doe, gies the questionin . . .

DOREEN: Tell ays whae it is! Tell ays ya fuckin philanderin bastard!

BOAB SENIOR: Ah'll nivir talk! . . . Edwards . . . O'Rourke . . . Gordon . . . Cropley and Duncah-ahn . . .

BOAB SENIOR wheezes, and DOREEN is concerned.

DOREEN: Ye awright, Boab? Mind yir asthma n that . . .

BOAB SENIOR: Aye . . . aye . . . keep up the questionin, Doreen . . . the crocodile clips . . . git the croc clips, Doe!

DOREEN reaches over BOAB SENIOR's shoulder and takes two clips from the mantelpiece and attaches them to BOAB SENIOR's nipples.

BLUEBOTTLE buzzes on the wall.

DOREEN snaps a much larger clip onto BOAB SENIOR's scrotum. He screams. She pushes the dildo in further.

DOREEN: Tell ays, Boab! Whae huv ye been seein!

BOAB SENIOR (*whispers*): Dolly Parton.

DOREEN: Whae? Ah cannae hear ye!

BOAB SENIOR: Dolly Parton!

DOREEN: That fuckin slut! Ah knew it! Whae else?

BOAB SENIOR: Anna Ford . . . n that Madonna . . . bit jist the once . . .

DOREEN: Scumbag! Bastard! Ya dirty fuckin prick! Ye ken whit this means!

BOAB SENIOR: No the shite, Doe, ah cannae eat yir shite . . .

Louder buzzing from the BLUEBOTTLE *on the wall.*

DOREEN: Ah'm gaunny shite in yir mooth, Boab Coyle! It's what wi baith want! Dinnae deny it!

BOAB SENIOR: Naw! Don't shite in ma mooth . . . don't . . . shite in ma mooth . . . shite in ma mooth . . . shite in ma mooth!

The BLUEBOTTLE *on the wall is buzzing with excitement, his long tongue swishing around his fly 'lips'. Unable to contain himself he springs from the wall and swarms around* BOAB SENIOR *and* DOREEN, *flying in and out of their ears.*

DOREEN: Shite! That bloody fly! (*The phone rings.*) Ah'll huv tae git that, Boab, it'll be oor Cathy. She'll jist pester us aw night if ah dinnae answer now. Don't go away!

She undoes the belt leaving the dildo in BOAB SENIOR*'s arse.*

BOAB SENIOR: Aw . . .

DOREEN *answers it. It is her daughter,* CATHY.

DOREEN: Hiya Cathy. How are ye doin, love? . . . Good . . . just the usual. You ken us. Dad's fine. How's the wee felly? . . . Aw, the wee lamb! N Jimmy? . . . Good. Listen love, wir jist sitting doon tae oor tea. Ah'll phone ye back in aboot half an hour and we'll huv a proper blether . . . right love . . . bye the now. (DOREEN *slyly reaches over for the* Evening News. BOAB *the* BLUEBOTTLE, *exhausted after his efforts, retreats to the wall, but* DOREEN *springs towards him and batters him with the paper. He falls down behind the sideboard.*) Got ye ya swine!

BOAB SENIOR: Nice one, Doe . . . that fly wis a bigger pest than young Boab . . . now gies that questionin again, Doe . . .

DOREEN: Right.

INT. FRONT ROOM. NIGHT.
We see the battered and broken body of BOAB, *groaning softly under the sideboard.*

Upstairs in the bedroom where we see BOAB SENIOR *and* DOREEN *fast asleep snoring loudly and contentedly.*

TITLES:
As the end titles appear, we see a football game in progress. The other side score.

A SOFT TOUCH

INT. PUBLIC HOUSE. LATE AFTERNOON.

An archetypal spartan pub on a Scottish Housing scheme. One guy, called JOHNNY, *who looks quite stoical, is playing the fruit machine and occasionally watching some other guys playing pool. The pub is not that busy but everybody who is there has been there for some time. There's an old drunk singing along to 'That's Life' on the karaoke machine. A pool player notices* JOHNNY *watching them.*

POOL PLAYER: Put yir name up, mate.

JOHNNY: Aye, ah might jist dae that. (*He moves from the fruit machine to the board and chalks up his initials, 'J.C.', anxious in case anybody moves in on the machine. He hurries back and starts to play.*) Hold ... nudge ...
A youngish, heavily pregnant woman in a checked blouse and leggings called CATRIONA *enters the pub. She is about to approach the bar and get a drink when she spots* JOHNNY *at the fruit machine and goes over to him. He sees her but makes out that he doesn't.*

He spins the fruit machine.

We then see JOHNNY's *face with* CATRIONA *looking over his shoulder in a predatory manner.*

JOHNNY *stands stiffly and stoically.*

CATRIONA: Awright, John. Still playin the bandit then, eh?

JOHNNY: Aye, looks like it, eh.

CATRIONA: No goat the money tae git ays a drink then, John?

JOHNNY *briefly shifts his attention from the fruit machine and looks her up and down.*

JOHNNY: You in the family wey again then, Catriona?

CATRIONA: Is it that obvious, Johnny?

> *In spite of* CATRIONA's *pregnancy,* JOHNNY *is obviously checking out her tits and arse and is mildly aroused. Wedding music starts up as* JOHNNY's *mind drifts.*

INT. HOTEL FUNCTION ROOM. AFTERNOON.

JOHNNY *and* CATRIONA *are standing behind the wedding cake. She is wearing a white wedding dress, but is obviously pregnant. The chapel is full of friends and relatives, some of whom are already pretty drunk. The band play 'Wonderwall' as we see a montage of wedding guest scenes.*

INT. HOTEL. EVENING.

It is a stark hotel function room; wooden dancefloor, formica tables, disco, bar, light projected against spinning crystal ball on the ceiling. JOHNNY *and* CATRIONA *are up on the floor alone doing the bridal dance to Oasis's 'Wonderwall'. Some old wifies coo and some boys cheer. There is an obvious gap between* JOHNNY's *side and* CATRIONA's *side, who are far wilder. We focus on one group of drunk youths. A group of youths snigger at the back:* ALAN, SKANKO *and* DEEK. *They are talking, unaware that* ALEC DOYLE *is watching them.*

ALAN: It's a good thing that perr auld Johnny gits huckled! Keeps the CSA oot ay your face, eh Deek? Mind the time ah hud it at Doogie Morrison's perty. You wir thaire n aw Sammy. Mind wi that Sonia! We swapped thum ower! That Sonia wisnae game at first but that dirty cow Catriona wis right intae it fae the stert!

> ALEC DOYLE *hears this and approaches.*

ALEC: What did you jist fuckin say the now? (ALAN *shrugs, but looks scared.*) Aye, you. What did you jist say the now?

30

ALAN *stand up and spreads his hands outward in a passive gesture.*

ALAN: Nowt, Alec . . . jist huvin a blether, eh . . . jist pished n talkin shite man . . . jist sayin . . .
ALEC *headbutts* ALAN *in the face and as he falls to the ground starts to systematically kick his ribs in.*

ALEC: Jist fuckin sayin, ur ye? Well ah'm jist fuckin well sayin this . . . (ALEC *continues his attack. There are a few shouts and screams, but most people just survey this scene casually.*) . . . n this . . .
. . . n this . . .
. . . that's whit ah'm jist fuckin sayin . . .
. . . what the fuck ur you jist sayin now? Eh!
When he runs out of steam, a drunk comes along and pats him on the back.

DRUNK: Well done, son. This husnae been a bad do but it wis missin something. A weddin needs a swedge tae make it go oaf right. Tradition n that.

ALEC (*to* JOHNNY): Sorry aboot that, Johnny. Ah ken these cunts are mates ay yours, bit thir no real mates. Thir wis nae respect fir you or ma sister. Yir faimlay now, Johnny. Any cunt thit fucks wi you, fucks wi me. Mind that. Any time some cunt gits lippy, you jist mind that.

INT. JOHNNY'S FLAT. MIDDAY.
The flat is local authority-owned, in a municipal housing scheme. It has very little furniture, but there is an ostentatiously large telly and video. It is occupied by JOHNNY, CATRIONA *and their baby,* CHANTEL, *whom* JOHNNY *is playing with.* CATRIONA *is watching the telly.*

INT. STAIR OF FLAT. AFTERNOON.
JOHNNY *and* CHANTEL *go downstairs.*

INT/EXT. OUTSIDE STAIR OF FLAT. AFTERNOON.
As JOHNNY *leaves the flat with* CHANTEL, *he comes across a shifty, hard-looking guy called* LARRY, *who is unloading goods from a van and taking them up the stairs.* LARRY *speaks quickly and sharply.*

JOHNNY: Awright, mate?

LARRY: Aye . . .

JOHNNY: Jist move intae Mrs Robertson's hoose?

    LARRY *looks warily at* JOHNNY.

LARRY: Aye ah ah'm. What's it tae you?

JOHNNY: Ah stey jist below ye. Doon the stairs fae ye, eh. Ye wantin a hand?

    LARRY *looks* JOHNNY *up and down, then gives an approving, predatory smile.*

LARRY: Cheers, mate. Ah'm Larry, by the way.

    He extends his hand, which JOHNNY *shakes.*

JOHNNY: Johnny.

LARRY: Nice one, Johnny.

INT. FLAT. EARLY EVENING.
CATRIONA *is getting herself made up to go out. She is overdone in the tacky glamour of a true skanker.* JOHNNY *is playing with* CHANTEL, *he is still dressed in his green supermarket overalls.*

JOHNNY (*to child*): There ye go, Chantel . . . oh, that wis a long day yir daddy hud the day. In the supermarket, Chantel, where they buy aw the nice things . . . (*He stands up from* CHANTEL's *playpen and turns to* CATRIONA. *He is concerned with the way she is dressed.*) Listen, Catriona, ah gave ye twenty bar tae go oot, tae git a brek fae the bairn. It's no that ah grudge it likes, it's jist that ah want tae ken whaire yir gaun. That's no too much tae ask, is it? Whaire's it yir gaun well?

CATRIONA: Oot, ah telt ye.

JOHNNY: Aye, bit whaire but?

CATRIONA: Ah sais oot. You telt ays tae go oot, so ah'm fuckin well gaun oot. Right?

JOHNNY: Bit dressed up like a fuckin tart!

CATRIONA *stands up and, with an expression of total scorn and withering contempt on her face, she makes for the door.*

CATRIONA: You don't get it, do ye?

CATRIONA *leaves.* JOHNNY *starts talking at* CHANTEL.

JOHNNY: See that, Chantel? That's your Ma! That!

INT. STAIRS IN FLAT. EARLY EVENING.

CATRIONA *meets* LARRY *on the stairs. They are flirtatiously checking each other out.*

LARRY: Awright doll? How's it gaun?

CATRIONA: No bad.

LARRY: You Johnny's bird?

CATRIONA: Aye. You must be the new guy.

LARRY: Aye, the name's Larry. Listen, doll, naebody ever tell you ye wir gorgeous? (CATRIONA *blushes stagily.*) Ah'm tellin ye. See if ye wir ma bird, ah widnae be lettin ye go oot dressed like that, no unless ah wis gaun oot wi ye!

CATRIONA: Aw aye?

LARRY: Too right. Ah'll huv tae huv a wee blether wi Johnny, pit um right oan one or two things. Mibee git a wee blether wi you n aw though, sometime, eh?

CATRIONA: Aye. Mibee.

They hold a gaze before smiling and departing. The

33

camera follows LARRY *to the stairbend. He pats his crotch.*

LARRY: Down, boy . . . phoah, ah'd fuckin gie thon piece one aw right. In a fuckin minute.

LARRY *turns and realises that he is outside* JOHNNY's *door. He looks briefly at it, then up the stairs to his own flat, before knocking.*

INT. FLAT. EARLY EVENING.

JOHNNY *answers the door excitedly, almost as if he expects* CATRIONA *to have changed her mind and come back. He sees that it's* LARRY.

LARRY: Awright, mate?

JOHNNY: No bad.

LARRY: Saw yir missus oan the wey oot. Thought ye might want a bit ay company, eh. Fancy a pint?

JOHNNY: Ah cannae . . . ah've goat the bairn . . . come in for a can if ye like.

LARRY *pushes into the flat with extreme haste, rubbing his hands.*

LARRY: Top gadgie, top gadgie.

JOHNNY *takes off his supermarket overall and throws it across a chair.*

EXT. STREETS. NIGHT.

CATRIONA *walks along the street on her way home.*

INT. JOHNNY'S FLAT. NIGHT.

CATRIONA *is banging on the door.* JOHNNY *lets her in. There are a few cans lying empty. She is obviously drunk. She is covered in love bites. He is distraught at her condition.*

JOHNNY: Shut the fuck up! Ye'll wake the fuckin bairn! Dae ye ken whit time it is! Ah've goat work the moarn! Whair's yir key? Whair ye been! WHIT'S THAT OAN YIR FUCKIN NECK!!

CATRIONA: Ootay ma fuckin face, ah'm burstin . . .

CATRIONA *pushes past him and goes to the toilet. While she is taking a pish,* JOHNNY *rummages through her bag and checks her purse. He is upset even further to find forty pounds in it. He confronts her as she emerges from the toilet.*

JOHNNY: What's this! Forty fuckin bar! Ah gave ye twenty bar cause ye wir skint, n ye come back wi forty! Whae gave ye this! Whae gave ye aw that oan yir neck!

CATRIONA: Somebody that wisnae you!

JOHNNY: Lit ays see yir fanny! Ah want tae check yir fanny fir spunk! Lit ays feel it!

CATRIONA: You come near me n ma brars'll be right doon here!

JOHNNY *moves towards her then hesitates.*

JOHNNY: Aye, well mibee yir brothers'll find oot one day that ah've goat mates n aw.

CATRIONA: What? What does that mean?

JOHNNY: Jist means thit ah've goat mates n aw.

CATRIONA: What fuckin mates huv you goat?

She looks and sees the empty cans. JOHNNY *looks a little uplifted.*

JOHNNY: Mates that you dinnae ken aboot. Mates close by.

CATRIONA: Whae? That Larry gadge up the stairs! Huh! Ye think that he'll dae anything! Huh!

JOHNNY: Mibee.

CATRIONA: Ye think cause yuv been knockin aboot wi him, that fuckin Larry, thit naebody kin touch ye? Well ah'll fuckin well touch ye! (CATRIONA *starts assaulting* JOHNNY *who backs away. She then moves to the bedroom.*) Huh! N' ah'll tell ye one thing, son, yir no sleepin wi me the night. You kin sleep doon here, oan the couch.

JOHNNY: Too fuckin right ah will. Ah'm no sleepin wi a fuckin hoor!

CATRIONA *looks at him witheringly and walks out of the room.* JOHNNY *looks hurt, then forces a look of determination.*

INT. LARRY'S FLAT. DAY.

LARRY *is soaping up in the shower singing along to Marc Bolan's 'Hot Love', taking pleasure in his good physical shape.*

EXT/INT. STAIRS OF FLAT. EARLY EVENING.

JOHNNY, *dressed in supermarket overalls, enters close and climbs stairs.*

EXT. JOHNNY'S FLAT. EARLY EVENING.

JOHNNY *turns the key to the door of the flat. On opening it he hears laughter and music.*

INT. FLAT. EARLY EVENING.

CATRIONA *and* LARRY *from upstairs are on the couch, sharing a bottle of vodka and some cans of Superlager.*

LARRY: The man himself! What aboot the workers then! Come oan n join us, mate, join the fuckin perty, eh!

JOHNNY (*to* CATRIONA): Whair's Chantel?

CATRIONA: Took hur doon tae your Ma's.

JOHNNY: When ur ye gaunny go doon n git hur!

LARRY: Hi! That's no the kind ay crack ye expect fae friends n neighbours! A wee fuckin perty! Goat tae be

36

fuckin social, eh!

JOHNNY: Aye, well she's no meant tae be fuckin social. (*They ignore him and watch the television.*) Do you care? Do you gie a fuck?

CATRIONA: Aye. Aye a do.

JOHNNY: Left that wee girl doon at me ma's.

CATRIONA: Aye, ah do!

JOHNNY: An ye? Well ah've a wee test fir ye – What wis she wearing?

CATRIONA: Charrise.

JOHNNY: If wis ne charrise it wis pink. Ye ken what that is?

CATRIONA: Aye. P-ink. Pink.

LARRY *winks at* CATRIONA, *who laughs loudly.*

JOHNNY: Ah'll fuckin well go doon fir hur ... git some fuckin tea, eh. (To LARRY *sarcastically.*) You want the story fir yir tea Larry?

LARRY: Ah'd love tae stay fir ma tae. That awright wi you Cat?

CATRIONA: Lovely.

JOHNNY: Right, ah'll go 'n git the tea in. N ah'll even git ye a video 'n all Larry.

LARRY: Bruce Willis – *Die Hard.*

JOHNNY: Right.

LARRY: Nice one, Johnny ... n pick up some mair tins n aw then ya cunt, wi'll be runnin a wee bit dry here soon, eh.

JOHNNY: What ... eh ... right.

LARRY: Johnny! Git us *Die Harder*

JOHNNY *exits to the loud sounds of laughter.*

EXT. STREETS/EXT. MOTHER'S STAIR. AFTERNOON.

JOHNNY *is walking to his mother's house. Kids are hanging*

around in the street outside his mother's stair.

EXT. MOTHER'S BACKGREEN. AFTERNOON.
JOHNNY *is visiting his mother with* CHANTEL. *His mother is a hard-faced chain-smoking woman with a pervading air of bitterness.*

MOTHER: So the Doaktir said tae cut doon oan the cigarettes, John. Ah jist turned roond n said tae him; it's only the fags that's keepin me gahn, that an seeing ma laddie settled doon properly. Eh mairried a hoor, ah telt him, a common person.

JOHNNY: Aye . . . bit . . .

MOTHER: Ye see, son, yir too much ay a soft touch. People see that in ye. Auld Soft Johnny . . . mind they used tae call ye that at the school?

JOHNNY: Naw . . . naw they didnae . . .

MOTHER: Come oan now, son! Ah mind! Ah mind awright. Weak, like yir faither.

JOHNNY: Naw ah'm no! Ah telt Alec Doyle what eh could dae wi his stuff! Telt um ah wisnae huvin that shite in ma hoose!

JOHNNY'S MOTHER *isn't listening.*

MOTHER: That wis the school. Oor Julie wis always good at the school. No you though. But that wis the school. Then came that hoor. That wis a waste ay time.

JOHNNY: Aye . . . bit then came Chantel. So it wisnae a waste ah time. So if it wisnae fir me gittin the gither wi Catriona, thir wouldnae huv been Chantel.

They look at CHANTEL, *who is playing on the carpet with her toys.*

MOTHER: Aye, she's a wee princess, right enough.

JOHNNY: So yuv goat tae see it that wey.

MOTHER: Aye, well, mibee.

38

INT. JOHNNY'S FLAT. EVENING.

JOHNNY *is alone with the baby,* CHANTEL, *in the council flat. There is a space where the video and television were. He hears the sounds of laughter coming from up the stairs. It is the voices of* LARRY *and* CATRIONA.

JOHNNY (*to* CHANTEL): Your mother darlin. That's her up thair. A fuckin hoor, that's what she is. A slut. She just steys maist nights up thair wi him now. Doesnae even bother aboot you.

INT. LARRY'S FLAT UPSTAIRS. EVENING.

LARRY *and* CATRIONA *are shagging on a mattress in their flat. There is a telly and a video which look like* JOHNNY*'s. Her legs are pinned high to the ceiling and she is crushed against a wall. Her face is pinched, tight and vicious.* LARRY*'s is sneering and contemptuous.*

LARRY: Yuv nivir fuckin been rode like this before, eh . . .
CATRIONA: Oh it's sair . . . oh . . . Larry . . . ah could fuckin well eat you . . .
LARRY: That's me doll . . . jist like fuckin chocolate, eh . . .

INT. FLAT DOWNSTAIRS. EVENING.

JOHNNY *and* CHANTEL.

JOHNNY: My ma wis right. She says her and her family, the fuckin Doyles wir rubbish, eh, Chantel. Well we're no rubbish, eh no darlin? No us. That's thaim up thair. Ma ma wis right aboot me n aw. She sais ah wis a soft touch. She sais that they saw ah wis a worker n they took a len ay me.

INT. FLAT UPSTAIRS. EVENING.
LARRY *and* CATRIONA.

CATRIONA: Oh Larry . . . no sae hard . . . it's sair . . .
LARRY: Naw . . . it's awright . . . the pole's fuckin well
    greased here, eh . . .

INT. JOHNNY'S DOWNSTAIRS. EVENING.
JOHNNY *and* CHANTEL.

JOHNNY: They broke in here, Chantel. Broke in and took
    away the telly n the video. Ah cannae leave anything
    in here now . . .
    . . . cannae even show ye yir Postman Pat video . . .

INT. FLAT UPSTAIRS. EVENING.
LARRY *and* CATRIONA.

CATRIONA: Oh . . . keep fuckin me . . .
LARRY: Till thir's silverware in Gorgie doll . . .

INT. JOHNNY'S FLAT. EVENING.
JOHNNY *sits in misery with* CHANTEL, *the noises which melt
into high orgasmic groans, all too audible to him. Then it
ceases.*

JOHNNY: You're different fae her, Chantel, you're a
    princess, eh hen. Yir daddy's wee Princess. Different
    fae that hoor!
    JOHNNY *hears the doorbell and is about to leave the
    bathroom.*
40

INT. LARRY'S FLAT. EVENING.
LARRY *is hammering a hole in his floor.*

INT. JOHNNY'S FLAT. LIVING-ROOM/CEILING. EVENING.
Plaster falling from the ceiling of JOHNNY*'s flat.* LARRY*'s face framed in the hole he has made in* JOHNNY*'s ceiling, he has a big grin on his face.*

INT. JOHNNY'S FLAT. LIVING-ROOM/CEILING. EVENING.
There is a cable with a plug attached to it swinging from the hole in the ceiling. JOHNNY *goes to the door.* LARRY *barges into the flat and moves past* JOHNNY. *He is wearing a T-shirt and tracksuit trousers.*

LARRY: Awright mate. Listen, ah need a wee favour, eh. They fuckin electric cunts huv only gone and cut ays oaf. (LARRY *moves quickly to the plug. He takes the plug and connects it into the socket where the TV and video used to be.*) That's me sorted oot!
JOHNNY: Eh?
LARRY: Ah've goat an extension block up the stairs. Jist needed a power point wi electric fae it, eh.
JOHNNY: That's ootay order, that's ma electricity!
JOHNNY *advances to unplug the flex, but* LARRY *blocks his path. He raises his right hand above his head and points downwards at* JOHNNY, *rocking on the balls of his feet as he speaks, like a football fan denouncing the rival supporters across the terraces.*
LARRY: See if you ivir touch that fuckin plug or switch, Johnny, you're fuckin well deid! Ah'm fuckin tellin ye! (JOHNNY*'s head falls.* LARRY *calms down a little and breaks into a smile.*) Listen, Johnny, you n me ur still mates, that's the wey ah see it. Forget everything thit's

41

happened, tae me we're still mates n that's that, eh. Ah mean, ah'll go halfers oan the fucking bills if that's whit yir worried aboot!

JOHNNY: Halfers, aye. Well your bills'll be a loat mair than mine cause ah've goat nowt left that uses electricity!

LARRY: What's that meant tae mean then, John?

LARRY's *face changes again as he stares* JOHNNY *down.*

JOHNNY: Nowt.

LARRY: Better fuckin no mean nowt. (LARRY *strolls across the room. His face changes from overt aggression to some kind of half-sneering, half-conspiratorial smile. He points upstairs.*) No bad ride though, eh, John? Ah mean, sorry tae huv tae move in thair. Jist one ay they things. She wis gantin oan it. (*He winks at* JOHNNY.) Gies a barry gam though, eh?

JOHNNY: Eh . . .

LARRY: Ever fucked it up the erse? (*Crosses one of his arms over the other one.*) Ah sterted giein it the message that wey, ah mean, ah'm no wantin it up the stick, eh no. Bairn daft, that cunt. Ah mean, once ye git a slag up the stick they think thit thuv goat thir hand in yir poakit fir the rest ay yir puff. Isnae ma fuckin scene, ah'll tell ye that fir nowt. Ah'll keep ma money! (LARRY *laughs loudly, oblivious to* JOHNNY's *dejection.*) Tell ye one thing though, John, ah hope yuv no goat that AIDS or nowt like that, cause see if ye huv, ye'd've gied it tae me by now. Ah nivir bother usin a rubber when ah shaft her up the stairs thair. No way; ah'd rather huv a fuckin wank, man.

JOHNNY: Naw, ah've no goat nowt like that.

LARRY: Jist as well, ya dirty wee cunt! Tell ye something else, Johnny . . . (LARRY *walks over and pats* CHANTEL's *head.*) . . . yuv goat me tae thank fir you keepin the bairn here. She wants it, bit ah keep sayin naw, even though you fuckin well ken n ah fuckin well ken, thit a bairn belongs wi its Ma. Bit naw, ah keep pittin the daft cunt oaf, cause ah'm no intae huvin bairns aroond the hoose. So it's thanks tae me yuv goat the bairn! Think aboot that the next time ye start makin accusations aboot other people!

Gaunny huv a mooth like her Ma that yin, eh! Good at suckin oan things! (*He laughs and slaps* JOHNNY *on the back.*) See the draw for the quarter-finals? The winners ay St Johnstone v Kilmarnock. At Easter Road likes. (LARRY *makes to leave and stops at the door, dropping his voice.*) One other thing, John, if ye want a poke at it again, jist gies a shout. A tenner tae you. Gen up likes.

We see CATRIONA *lying in the bed upstairs, absolutely fucked.*

EXT. STREETS NEAR D.I.Y. SHOP. DAY.
JOHNNY *pushing* CHANTEL *along in go-cart, past a small row of shops. He is on his way to his* MOTHER's *house. We observe various vignettes happening in the background as* JOHNNY *walks past.*

EXT. MOTHER'S FLAT DOOR. DAY.
JOHNNY's MOTHER *takes* CHANTEL *and hands* JOHNNY *a toolbag.*

EXT. STREET NEAR SHOPS. DAY.
JOHNNY *is heading back towards his own flat with the toolbag. As he stops off at the D.I.Y. shop, we pick up on some of the background action as it has progressed from the last time* JOHNNY *passed.*

INT. JOHNNY'S FLAT. LIVING-ROOM. DAY.
JOHNNY *walks into his living-room and yanks the cable down from the hole in the ceiling.*

INT. JOHNNY'S FLAT/CEILING. DAY.
We see JOHNNY *through the hole in the ceiling.*
JOHNNY *opens the toolbag and takes out a hammer. He begins to block up the hole, whacking nails into the ceiling.*

JOHNNY: Fuck you!

EXT. STREET. EARLY EVENING.
JOHNNY *is walking down the road on his own, carrying a Safeways plastic bag.*

EXT/INT. STAIRS OF MOTHER'S FLAT. EARLY EVENING.
JOHNNY *is on his way home from work. He enters the stairs to find* CATRIONA *is standing in the doorway to the backgreen. She walks into the close, smiling at him and wearing a short skirt and a tight top.*

CATRIONA: Hi, Johnny . . .
JOHNNY: What dae you want?
CATRIONA: Just tae talk, Johnny . . .
 She moves into the backgreen.

EXT. MOTHER'S BACKGREEN. EARLY EVENING.

CATRIONA: C'mere the now Johnny . . .
 JOHNNY *follows her out but it is a trap and he is set*
44

upon by LARRY *who administers a brutal kicking.*
CATRIONA *cheers him on.*

LARRY: Ye took the fuckin pish, Johnny. Nae cunt takes the fuckin pish oot ay me!

CATRIONA: Blooter that bastard! Kill the cunt! Oor fuckin electric! It wis oor fuckin electricity! He's goat ma fuckin bairn! His fuckin auld hoor ay a mother's goat ma fuckin bairn! (*They give* JOHNNY *a good doing, then depart, leaving him on the ground.* CATRIONA *continues to goad him.*) Go back tae yir fuckin Ma! Lick yir Ma's piss-flaps ya fuckin cunt!

As CATRIONA *walks away,* JOHNNY *reaches up to grab a washing pole as he staggers to his feet. He checks through his pockets and, realising the cash is still there, he punches the air in triumph.*

JOHNNY: So that's the best ye can fuckin dae! Ye didnae even find ma money ya daft cunts!

JOHNNY *begins to stagger towards the stairs.*

INT. SUPERMARKET. DAY.
Visual montage of shoppers and shopgirls.

INT. PUB. DAY.
JOHNNY *plays the bandit.*

INT. LARRY'S NEW FLAT. EVENING.
There is a party going on in LARRY's *new flat. It is all very rowdy. There are a lot of wasters, drugs, etc.* LARRY *is on the couch with a young girl, having flirty blow-backs with a large joint.* CATRIONA *is pregnant and making a big thing about putting empty cans in the binliner.*

LARRY: When ah make love tae a lassie, ah nivir use a condom. That's me, eh. What aboot you, do you

45

eywis use a condom whin ye make love?
The girl shrugs.
LARRY *turns to* CATRIONA.

LARRY: Whae asked you tae open yir fuckin mooth! Fat cunt!

CATRIONA: Fuckin . . . ah'm fuckin gaun! Right! (*She looks around furiously, pointing at the girl.*) Fuck that slut if ye fuckin well want! Ah dinnae fuckin care!
She storms off, slamming the door behind her.

LARRY: Fuck off ya fat cunt! (*He turns to the girl.*) Fuck that sow! Dinnae ken whae's fuckin bairn it is, bit it isnae mine. Ah want tae git ma heid doon in a bit. Ye comin through?
She nods.

INT. PUBLIC HOUSE. LATE AFTERNOON.
We are back in the pub where we started. JOHNNY *is playing the bandit and* CATRIONA *is with him.*

POOL PLAYER: Right, mate! Yir oan.
JOHNNY: Right.
    JOHNNY *goes over and breaks. Nothing goes down and the other player takes the table.*
    JOHNNY *is distracted by* DIANA *who has entered the bar with her mates and is getting a round in.* CATRIONA *looks on jealously as* JOHNNY *waves at* DIANA. *The girls giggle and nudge each other.*
    JOHNNY *goes back to the fruit machine.*
POOL PLAYER: Hi mate.
    JOHNNY *goes to the pool table, then back to* CATRIONA, *after taking a shot.*
JOHNNY: So where's Larry these days?
CATRIONA: Fuck knows. Eh's stayin wi some fuckin slut.
    JOHNNY *moves to the pool table.*

JOHNNY: (*under his breath*) It's no fuckin like um right enough.

CATRIONA: As soon as he found oot ah wis pregnant eh just fucked off. (*She takes a drag from her fag.*) Listen Johnny, ye want tae go oot the night?

JOHNNY *looks flabbergasted at this audacity.*

CATRIONA: Up the toon likes? Up the Bull and Bush? We wir good the gither Johnny eh? Mind. Everybody said so.

JOHNNY *looks bemused at this.*

CATRIONA: Mind the bandit at the Bull and Bush, Johnny?

JOHNNY: Aye, it was a good bandit right enough.

CATRIONA: Dae ye want tae go then Johnny? Eh?

JOHNNY: Aye. Awright.

DIANA *and her friends look puzzled as* JOHNNY *and* CATRIONA *sit down together by the pool table.*

THE ACID HOUSE

EXT. PUBLIC PARK IN HOUSING SCHEME. LATE AFTERNOON. *It is a cool summer's day. It has been strangely hot for Scotland. A young couple are walking arm-in-arm. The girl, KIRSTY, has the boy COCO's, arm tightly. She is intense, he is slightly distracted.*

KIRSTY: Susan was sayin tae ays that they wir thinkin ay huvin thir reception at the new function suite at Easter Road. Ah goes: dinnae tell Coco you'll be huvin it thair or he'll want yin in aw!

COCO: Aye . . . right. That wis a cracker at Rez last weekend but, eh.

KIRSTY: Aye . . . they say that ye can huv a perty for up tae three hundred people thair.

COCO: Naw . . . ye kin git upwards ay twelve thousand at Rezurection. Inglistion showgrounds, eh.

KIRSTY: Naw, ah wis meanin the function suites at Easter Road. ·

COCO: Aw right . . . bit Rezurection bit, that Bass Generator boy wis sound, eh . . .

KIRSTY: Bit see at they function suites, for weddings n that, ye dinnae pey for the place, but ye huv tae take thair buffet. Ye git a choice but.

COCO: . . . ah mean you ken me, ah'm no intae aw that redneck hardcore shite. It's aw wankers fae places like Cumbernauld n Livvy whair thir's nowt tae dae thit go fir that. Ah'm a city boy, a Hibs boy, a soul boy. Ah sais that tae Skanko. But ah huv tae admit, Rez wis a wee bit special.

KIRSTY: Aye, wisnae bad.

COCO: Fuckin well sufferin a bit now but, eh.

EXT. STREET/PUB. TWILIGHT.
COCO *and* KIRSTY *enter a large, cavernous, scheme pub.*

INT. PUB. LATE AFTERNOON.
COCO *goes to the toilet leaving* KIRSTY *to get the drinks in and find seats.*

INT. PUB TOILET. LATE AFTERNOON.
COCO *is in the toilet. He opens a fag pocket and tips out a tab of acid with a big, bright face on it.*

INT. PUB. LATE AFTERNOON.
KIRSTY *is sitting near the corner near a couple who have a toddler with them.* COCO *joins her. The toddler on his mother's lap at the next table is looking over at them.*

KIRSTY: Aw . . . look at that wee soul.

COCO: Shouldnae huv bairns in a pub.

KIRSTY: Ah think it's nice. It means that people can get oot.

COCO: Ye can get oot easier withoot fuckin bairns but, eh. Couldnae handle aw that shite. No intae bairns, eh.
(COCO *is starting to act a bit disorientated.*) Whoah . . .

KIRSTY: Well, if everybody wis like that, thir wouldnae be any human race.

COCO: Ha ha ha. That suits me. It's aw fucked anywey. Ye live, ye die, that's it. (COCO *looks over at the family.*) Fuck huvin bairns aroond! In a fucking scheme pub!

KIRSTY: Keep yir voice doon, Coco!

52

COCO: Nuht ah'll no keep ma voice doon. How should ah!
Ah've telt ye, ah'm no intae aw that straight-peg shite!
This is what this is aw aboot. Me n you gittin fuckin
married. Well ah'm no gittin married.

KIRSTY: Bit Skanko n Leanne ur gittin engaged.

COCO: Skanko's Skanko. Leanne's Leanne. Ah'm Coco,
you're Kirsty. That's that.

KIRSTY: Aye, bit ye couldnae call Skanko a straight-peg.

COCO (*downing drink*): Look ah've telt ye before, dinnae
start nippin ma heid . . . look, ah've goat tae nash. Ah
sais tae Davie ah'd go ower tae his bit. C'moan. Ah'll
git ye doon the road . . .

KIRSTY: Aye . . . but . . .

COCO: Listen, doll, ah sais ah've goat tae nash. Ah jist
dropped one ay they supermario's in the bogs and it's
startin tae kick in goodstyle. Davie n Goagsie wir
sayin it's the ragest acid thuv hud . . .

KIRSTY: Aw, Coco . . .

COCO: S'awright but, ah kin handle ma fuckin drugs. Jist
dinnae heidfuck ays right now, eh, doll. Ah've goat tae
git oot intae the air, eh. Bit ah'll come roond tae
your's the morn, doll. C'mon, ah've goat tae nash
here. Whoah . . . business fuckin gear . . .

KIRSTY *complies in a surly fashion as they leave the pub.*

INT. JENNY'S FLAT. HALL. DAY.

EMMA *and* JENNY *are two middle-class, professional women
in their late twenties. They are obviously pregnant. They are
in the hallway of* JENNY'*s flat as* EMMA *gets ready to leave.*

EMMA: God, Jen! Look at us!

JENNY: Actually, I'd rather not . . . a pretty bad case of
sperm overdose.

EMMA: You know, I sometimes wish, looking back to that

53

cold winter's evening, that I'd given Iain that blow-job instead.

They laugh. RORY WESTON, *a worried-looking man in his late twenties/early thirties arrives home.* RORY *pats* JENNY*'s and* EMMA*'s bellies and goes into the living-room.*

EMMA: How's Rory coping with all this?

JENNY: The same way Rory copes with everything. Makes all the correct noises but doesn't actually do anything except stand around and irritate me. I don't mind him being useless, if he didn't profess to have a view on everything.

EMMA: I'm sure his heart's in the right place.

JENNY: The centre of his chest, yes.

INT. JENNY'S FLAT. LIVING-ROOM. DAY.

RORY *is in the living-room. He has a copy of a parenting magazine.*

EXT. PARK/ROUNDABOUT. NIGHT.

COCO BRYCE *is standing on a moving roundabout. He has done a lot of acid. The sky seems to have split open, with a translucent glow emanating from it.* COCO *feels rain on his face and hears thunder and sees lightning. He is struck by it and falls face down onto the path.*

COCO (*stunned scream*): Fuckin . . .

EXT. PARK/ROUNDABOUT. NIGHT.

COCO *is tripping. He is spinning on a roundabout. He falls to his feet, still on the moving roundabout.*

COCO (*v.o.*): Who?
What?
Where?
How?
What am ah?
Coco Bryce. Brycey fae Pilton: one ay the Hibs boys, a fuckin top boy! Coco Fuckin Bryce ya radge cunts!

EXT. PARK/ROUNDABOUT. NIGHT.
A flash of lightning. X-ray of COCO*'s head and body while he is spinning . . . we see an acid green glow in his stomach that is starting to run through his veins.*

COCO: Am ah deid? So this is fuckin deid! Well fuck that: Coco fuckin Bryce . . . this gear, it isnae real. Eftir ah come doon that's me finished wi acid!
More lightning flashes.

INT. HALLWAY OF FLAT. NIGHT.
RORY WESTON *is in the hallway of his flat. As he puts down the receiver of the telephone the source of his worry becomes apparent from the screams coming from the front room; his girlfriend,* Jenny, *has gone into labour. The sounds of a violent electrical storm can be heard from the outside.*

JENNY: Fucking hell . . . !
RORY: Hang on, Jen! They're on their way!
RORY *moves into the front room where* JENNY *is sitting on the sofa in distress. It is soaked with her waters. He crushes her hand in his.*
JENNY: It's so fucking sore, this is fucking killing me, Rory! I'm fucking dying here!
RORY: Easy, Jen, easy, there we go . . .

EXT. STREETS. NIGHT.
An ambulance races through the streets.

INT. BACK OF AMBULANCE VAN. NIGHT.
FELIX *and* RORY *are with* JENNY *in the back of the*
ambulance. TAM *is up front, driving.*

FELIX (*shouting to* TAM): Stop! It's happening now!
RORY: It can't happen now! We're in the Meadows in the
    middle of a storm!
TAM (*to* FELIX): Right, Felix.
    TAM *stops the van and joins them in the back.*
FELIX (*to* JENNY): Nae hassle love, just keep breathing
    intae this: just a bit ay gas an air. Push, hen, push.
RORY: Jen, I thought we agreed that we wouldn't get into
    this nitrous oxide thing on principle. . . . (FELIX *looks*
    at him witheringly. While this is going on, JENNY *is*
    pushing.) . . . I mean . . . it just makes the woman
    woozy and does nothing for the pain. Another form of
    patriarchal social control, I think we agreed.
FELIX: I don't think this is the time, sir. . . .

EXT. PARK. NIGHT.
There is a loud noise and a crackling and shaking as the
ambulance is struck by lightning.

INT. AMBULANCE. NIGHT.
JENNY *rips off her mask and lets out a scream.*

FELIX: . . . what the fuck . . .
RORY: What was that?
TAM: Felix! Is everything awright?
56

FELIX: It's better than that Tam . . . it's comin!

INT/EXT. PARK/ROUNDABOUT. LATE NIGHT.
COCO *is still spinning on the roundabout.*

COCO: Aw, this is nowt tae fuckin dae wi me!
Colin Stuart Bryce!
*Through a blur we see a montage of several flashback
scenes of* COCO*'s life; the voices floating in and out of the
picture, intercut with shots of blood flowing, x-rays, brain
scans, heat scans, blood cells, baby in womb.*

EXT. FOOTBALL GROUND. AFTERNOON.
COCO*'s face in twisted sneer looking over to rival fans as
crowd in background sing 'Hibees here, Hibees there, Hibees
every fuckin where.'*

INT. FRONT ROOM OF HOUSE. DAY.
A hangdog young COCO *looks on as his mother explains to
him.*

MOTHER: Dad's comin back tae us, Colin, dinnae be feart,
son, yir Ma widnae lit um hurt us again. Ah widnae
lit um back in the hoose unless he'd changed, son . . .

INT. CHAPEL. DAY.
A priest, his face twisted in a sneering smile, is giving COCO
communion, the 'bread' looking strangely like a tab of acid.

57

INT. FRONT ROOM OF HOUSE. EVENING.
COCO'S FATHER *is turning his attention from the television to shout at his son.*

FATHER: Yi'll dae is yir fuckin well telt, Colin, yuh wee cunt! Ah sais twinty fuckin Regal! Now! Move it!

INT. PUBLIC HOUSE. EVENING.
A group of young guys, including COCO *and friends,* SKANKO *and* ANDY *and another casual, all high on adrenaline, come into the city-centre pub.*

ANDY (*slapping* COCO *on the back in a gesture of camaraderie*): Ran these fuckin Hun bastards the day, eh? You're a tidy cunt, mate. Coco, is it no? Welcome tae the family. (*To the other assembled football casuals.*) Coco here boys, fucking main man, ah'm telling yis!

INT. NIGHTCLUB. NIGHT.
This is a typical feel-good club, with garagey/soul happy-house music, an even male to female ratio and everyone is E'd up. COCO *is in the chill-out zone talking to* KIRSTY, *who is chewing gum to avoid grinding her teeth.*

COCO: Kirsty, ah really like ye, ken?
KIRSTY: Aye, ah really like you n aw.
COCO: Ah mean, ah'm no that much good it talking like this, bit ye ken whit ah mean likesay, you n me, ken?
KIRSTY: Aye. Ah love you tae.

EXT. ROUNDABOUT. NIGHT.
COCO *falls down from his knees . . . he hangs over the edge of the roundabout . . . his head over the edge and his arms*

stretched out as if he is trying to grab something.

EXT. PARK/ROUNDABOUT. NIGHT.
COCO'*s transition into* BABY COCO.

COCO: Thir's gaunny be some fuckin changes aroond here
     ya cunts! A cunt that messes is a cunt that dies! Coco
     Bryce!
     He emerges, as a baby, in the ambulance.

INT. BACK OF AMBULANCE. NIGHT.

FELIX: It's a beauty!
TAM: A wee laddie for ye, hen, eh's a cracker n aw.
RORY: Look, Jen, he's wonderful!
BABY COCO (*v.o.*): What's the fuckin score ya cunts?
     TAM *slaps* BABY COCO *on the back and he lets out a
     loud, wrenching scream.*

EXT. PARK/ROUNDABOUT. NIGHT.
COCO *is lying upside down on the roundabout, with rain in
his face, crying like a baby . . .*

INT. HOSPITAL. DAY.
*A young man, identified as Colin Bryce, is lying on a bed,
behaving like a newborn baby. The ward television set is on.*
COCO *is being examined by a* DOCTOR *and a* NURSE.

DOCTOR CALLAGHAN: The waters are very muddy here.
     Struck by lightning on top of all this LSD his friends
     say he'd taken. I'm very doubtful as to whether this is

59

drug psychosis. But if it is, it's the worst case I've ever seen.

NURSE BOYD: I think he's trying to communicate with us. He's incapable of doing anything for himself, so when he needs food or the toilet he just screams more.

DOCTOR CALLAGHAN: Hmm ... like a baby ...

INT. JENNY'S FLAT. AFTERNOON.

JENNY *is preparing to breast-feed the baby, whom she's called* TOM. RORY *is looking on.*

JENNY: He's a little darling, what are you? Mummy's little darling boy!

BABY COCO (*off*): Phoa, ya cunt ye! This'll dae me! You've goat some pair ay fuckin jugs oan you right enough, doll.

RORY: How's Tom? How's little Tom-Tom?

BABY COCO (*off*): Coco ya radge cunts! Coco Bryce! CCS! Hibs Boys smash all opposition!

JENNY *pulls out a breast and puts her nipple into* BABY COCO's *mouth.*

JENNY: You're hungry today, aren't you!

BABY COCO (*off*): Phoah, ya fucker! This'll dae me! Ma name's Tom! Coco Bryce, who he?

RORY: He seems to be enjoying himself. Look at him! It's almost obscene!

BABY COCO (*off*): What's it goat tae dae wi you, ya specky cunt! Git tae fuck!

JENNY (*to* RORY): Jealous?

RORY: Don't be silly ... well ... I suppose so. The books are right. The male parent does feel excluded from the mother-baby bonding process. That might be an interesting one for me to air at the Men's Group tonight. You don't mind me going along, do you?

JENNY: No, you go if you want. Tom and I will amuse

ourselves. Won't we, Tom?

JENNY *lifts* BABY COCO *up and kisses his plump stomach making quacking noises.*

BABY COCO (*off*): Lower, ya big pump-up-the-nickers! Git your fuckin gums roond it!

JENNY: He's so lovely!

INT. HOSPITAL. AFTERNOON.
Close up of hands rolling a joint pull out to reveal that two of COCO's *mates,* ANDY *and another casual,* SKANKO, *have come to visit him on the ward.*

ANDY (*to* SKANKO): Fuckin shame, man. Coco's fucked. Jist lyin thair greetin like a bairn, eh.

SKANKO: Tell ays that's Coco Bryce lyin thair, man.
NURSE BOYD *approaches them.*

NURSE BOYD: Try to talk to him about some of the things you did together, some of the things he'd be interested in. (ANDY *looks bemused and* STEVIE *starts sniggering and shaking his head.*) You know, like discos and pop, that sort of thing.

ANDY: Aye, right! (*They laugh.*) Eh, ye missed yirsel the other day thair, Coco. The semi, ken? Wi wir waiting fir they Aberdeen cunts at Haymarket, eh. Booted fuck ootay the cunts man, chased thum back doon tae the station, back oantae the train, doon the fuckin tracks the loat! Polis jist fuckin well standing thair n aw, didnae ken what tae fuckin well dae, eh no. How good wis it, Stevie?

SKANKO: Fuckin barry ya cunt! Couple ay the boys goat lifted though: Gary, Mitzy n that crew. (*They look at the unresponsive, crying* COCO *for a second, before nervously carrying on.*)

N ye missed yirsel at Rezurection n aw, Coco.

That wis too mad. How radge wir they snowballs,
Andy?

ANDY: Mental! Ah thought they wir a bit smacky, but this
cunt wis up aw night. Ah jist wanted tae spraff n
gouch . . .

SKANKO: It's nae fuckin use, man, eh cannae even hear us,
like.

ANDY: This is fuckin too radge, man, cannae handle aw
this shite, eh.

INT. BEDROOM. NIGHT.

RORY *and* JENNY *are making love for the first time since*
JENNY *returned home with the baby. They start warily, but
then get into it and are really going for it.* BABY COCO *is
standing up in the pen, partly unseen in the shadows. He is
watching them.*

BABY COCO (*off*): Phoah, ya dirty cunts! Doggy style n aw!
RORY *sees the outline of the baby standing up in its cot.
He becomes distracted.*

JENNY: What is it, Rory? What the fuck is it!

RORY: The baby . . . it was like it was standing up,
watching us!

JENNY: Don't be so bloody stupid! C'mon, Rory, fuck me!

RORY: I can't . . . I mean . . . not with the baby in the
same room . . .

JENNY: For God's sake!

RORY: I'm sorry, Jen . . . it's just . . . I've been on paternity
leave to be with you and the baby . . . but I just feel
so redundant. I know it's natural . . . it's just . . .

JENNY (*turning away*): Oh, shut up and go to sleep.
Discuss it in your stupid fucking group!

RORY (*more to himself than* JENNY*'s back*): That group

provides an invaluable support network . . .

A close-up of the baby in his cot, obviously masterbating and climaxing.

INT. HOSPITAL. EVENING.

KIRSTY *visits* COCO *on the ward. He has made more progress.*

KIRSTY: Awright, Coco?

COCO: Caw-lin.

KIRSTY: Aye, Coco Bryce.

COCO: Co-co.

KIRSTY: Shanko n Leanne's set a date tae git mairried. That's what ah heard anywey. They wir engaged, mind?

COCO: Engaged.

KIRSTY: Ye dinnae do ye? Mind we wir gauuny git engaged? Mind we wir engaged? You wir jist gauuny git the ring?

COCO: Engaged.

KIRSTY: That's right, Colin and Kirsty. Engaged.

COCO: Caw-lin an Kirs-ty. Engage.

KIRSTY *sits over* COCO *and smiles at him.* COCO *rises and pushes his mouth towards her breasts and starts sucking and biting at them through her T-shirt.*

KIRSTY: Git the fuck offay ays! No here! No now!

She pushes him away. COCO *starts to cry due to the sharpness in her voice.* DOCTOR CALLAGHAN *enters.*

DOCTOR CALLAGHAN: Oh . . . oh . . . oh . . . come on now, come on now . . . there there . . . there there.

(*She soothes* COCO, *and takes* KIRSTY *aside.*) You see, Miss, you must remember that your boyfriend has become like a child, but he's accumulating knowledge at such a rapid rate, it's perfectly feasible that he could be completely normal again before too long. The problem, of course, is that he will in some ways be different from the Colin Bryce you knew.

63

KIRSTY: How?

DOCTOR CALLAGHAN: Well, he will have forgotten all his life experiences, forgotten all the good and the bad things he's done that have shaped him. In a sense, Colin is like a blank piece of paper waiting to be coloured in by the people close to him. This means that they must exercise responsibility.

KIRSTY: Aye, well ah'm gaunny keep um away fae they mates ay his in the casuals. And away fae drugs n aw . . . n before this happened, we wir gaunny git engaged. Ah didnae think ah wis up fir it at the time, wi him bein, like, a vegetable, but ah kin make him better. Ah still want tae git married tae Coco.

DOCTOR CALLAGHAN: You're a very brave girl, Kirsty. But you won't be alone, you'll have all the professional help in the rehabilitation process you and Colin require.

KIRSTY: That's awright then, well.

INT. BEDROOM. MORNING.

BABY COCO's room. JENNY enters and is horrified to smell alcohol from the cot.

BABY COCO (off): We do not carry hatchets, we do not carry chains, we only carry straws, to suck our lemonade . . . oh ya cunt ye, that vino wis strong. Cannae bevvy as much as ah used tae, no as a sprog . . .

JENNY: Tom! Oh God!

JENNY mops up the alcohol sick in the cot.

BABY COCO (off): Nivir goat cleaned up like this before, eh.

JENNY: It has to be Rory! He's flipped! Surely not . . . (Turns to BABY COCO.) It was bad daddy who did it,

64

wasn't it, Tom? Well whoever it was, I'm not going to let anybody hurt my little Tom-Tom, am I? We're going away, Tom, were going away to mummy's mummy, to granny down in Cheadle.

BABY COCO (*off*): Git tae fuck, ya daft sow! Ah'm gaun naewhair. Ah'm no yir bairn! Ah'm Coco Bryce! Goat tae pit this daft cunt in the picture!

JENNY: That's in Manchester, isn't it, Tom-Tom? Yes it is! Yes it is! And she'll be so pleased to see us! Yes she will! Will will will! *She smothers the baby's doughy cheek with kisses.*

BABY COCO: Look, eh, Jenny . . . (JENNY *freezes as she hears the words coming in a rasping, unnatural crackle from the baby's mouth.*)

(*Off*) Yuv done it now, ya daft cunt. Stey cool. Dinnae freak this sow oot.

JENNY: You spoke! Tom! You spoke!

BABY COCO *stands up in his cot as* JENNY *sways unsteadily.*

BABY COCO: Look, sit doon, eh, sit down. (JENNY *obeys in silent shock.*) You'd better no say nowt tae nae cunt aboot this, right? Eh, I mean, mother, they would not understand. Ah'm a sortay phenomenon, ah've goat eh, special intelligence n that. Right?

(*off*) Thank fuck fir aw they *Star Wars* videos ah used tae watch.

(*spoken*) They'd want tae take ays away!

JENNY: Never! I'd never let them take my Tom away! This is incredible! My little Tom! A special baby! But how, Tom? Why? Why us? Why you?

BABY COCO: Jist the way it goes eh, nae cunt kens. I mean, it's my destiny, mother.

JENNY: Oh Tom!

She scoops the child up in her arms.

EXT. BOTANIC GARDENS.

JENNY *has taken* BABY COCO *out to the hot house in the gardens*

BABY COCO: Aye, right! Eh listen, Ma, eh, Jenny, one or two wee things. The scran, eh, the food. It's no good. I want what grown ups get, but no aw that veggie shite yous eat.

JENNY: Well Rory and I believe . . .

BABY COCO: Ah couldnae gie a fuck what you an Rory believe . . . ah mean, youse have no right to deny me my free choice.

JENNY: You're right, Tom. You're obviously intelligent enough to articulate your own needs and we must respect that. Tell me . . . how is it you talk like that . . . I mean, in that accent?

BABY COCO: Ah picked things up. Top boy, eh.

JENNY: That's very good, Tom, but you shouldn't talk like that. You should have more positive role models. Try to be like somebody else.

BABY COCO: Like fuckin Rory, for instance?

JENNY: Well, maybe not . . .

BABY COCO: Sound. Ah'm a wee bit hungry though, eh.

JENNY: Oh, I'll take you through to the kitchen and we'll prepare something.

BABY COCO: Eh, ah wis thinkin mibee, a wee bit mair ay the tit n that . . .

JENNY: Oh, yes . . . right . . .

EXT. MONTAGE. MORNING.

KIRSTY *takes* COCO *to the park, then out shopping for clothes.*

EXT. STREET NEAR EASTER ROAD STADIUM. AFTERNOON.
JENNY *has* BABY COCO *strapped to her in her baby carrier.*
She is taking him to the match. Crowds are milling around.

JENNY (*whispering to baby*): I don't see why we have to
    come into the city on Saturday. We could have gone
    to the park.
BABY COCO: Fuck that. What is it wi posh cunts n parks?
    Lits git drink. Specky's oan the pish.
JENNY: You're absolutely right Tom. If Rory can do it,
    fuck em.
BABY COCO: Fuckin suren ah'm right. In here. C'mon.
    Nash.
JENNY: God, Tom, you take in everything.
    They go to the pub.

INT. PUB. AFTERNOON.
It is a crowded pub full of Hibs fans. KIRSTY *and* COCO *sit
in a corner. The fans are singing.*
KIRSTY: They've been at the football.
COCO: I want a scarf.
KIRSTY: Listen, Colin, football's just for silly wee laddies
    that never grow up. You're a full grown man. Aren't
    you?
COCO: Yes.
BABY COCO: There's the boys. If ah ken thaim, thill huv a
    squad planted in the away end tae start flingin
    punches and divertin the polis, while the main squad
    surge forward.
JENNY: Fighting!
BABY COCO: Aye. No want tae git huckled straight away.
    COCO *followed by* KIRSTY, *approaches* BABY COCO *and*
    JENNY. COCO *is fascinated by the baby.*
KIRSTY: He's lovely. How old is he?

67

JENNY: I sometimes have to ask myself that. COCO touches
the baby's face.

BABY COCO: Dinnae touch what ye cannae afford, you
cunt!

COCO: It's a nice baby.

KIRSTY: That's right, he's lovely. Really beautiful.

BABY COCO: That cunt looks like . . . me!

COCO *extends his hand to* BABY COCO.

BABY COCO: C'mon! Gie's it! Gie's it!

COCO *grabs* BABY COCO'*s hand and starts holding it
tightly. Both youth and child seem to be having some
kind of seizure as an energy crackles between them and
we see them both in x-ray.*

COCO: *Hibeeeeeeeees!!*

The Acid House

FILM FOUR INTERNATIONAL
Presents
A PICTURE PALACE NORTH & UMBRELLA
Production
A PAUL MCGUIGAN Film
Made with the support of Yorkshire Media Production
Agency, Scottish Arts Council National Lottery Fund,
Glasgow Film Fund
Based on the short stories from *The Acid House* by Irvine
Welsh
Starring
Ewen Bremner, Kevin McKidd, Martin Clunes, Jemma
Redgrave and Maurice Roëves as God
Costume Designers Pam Tait and Lynn Aitken
Production Designers Richard Bridgland and Mike Gunn
Director of Photography Alasdair Walker
Editor Andrew Hulme
Screenplay by Irvine Welsh
Produced by David Muir and Alex Usborne
Directed by Paul McGuigan

The Acid House Cast

The Granton Star Cause

Boab	Stephen McCole
God	Maurice Roëves
Kev	Garry Sweeney
Evelyn	Jenny McCrindle
Tambo	Simon Weir
Grant	Iain Andrew
Parkie	Irvine Welsh
Barman	Pat Stanton
Boab Snr	Alex Howden
Doreen	Ann Louise Ross
PC Cochrane	Dennis O'Connor
Sgt Morrison	John Gardner
Workmates	William Blair
	Garry McCormack
	Malcolm Shields
Rafferty	Stewart Preston

A Soft Touch

Johnny	Kevin McKidd
Catriona	Michelle Gomez
Alec	Tam Dean Burn
Larry	Gary McCormack
Pool Player	Scott Imrie
Alan	Niall Greig Fulton
Deek	William Blair
Skanko	Cas Harkins
Drunk	Maurice Roëves
Chantel (Baby)	Morgan Simpson
Chantel (Toddler)	Marnie Kidd
Mother	Alison Peebles

Diana	Joanne Riley
New Girl	Sarah Gudgeon
Wendy	Katie Echlin
Pub Singer	William 'Giggs' McGuigan

The Acid House

Coco	Ewen Bremner
Rory	Martin Clunes
Jenny	Jemma Redgrave
Kirsty	Arlene Cockburn
Emma	Jane Stabler
Priest	Maurice Roëves
CoCo's Father	Doug Eadie
CoCo's Mother	Andrea McKenna
Felix the Paramedic	Billy McElhaney
Tam the Driver	Ricky Callan
Nurse Boyd	Stephen Docherty
Dr Callaghan	Barbara Rafferty
Andy	Ronnie McCann
Skanko	Cas Harkins
Casting Consultant	Carolynne Sinclair Kidd

The Acid House / A Soft Touch Production

Production Manager Sara Barr
Production Co-ordinators Laura Cochrane, Nic Murison
Production Runner Bobby Seiler
Location Manager Fiona Winning
Location Assistants Jim Dunn, Donald Mackinnon
Winniebago Driver Brian Morrison
1st Assistant Directors Neil Calder, Bill Clark
2nd Assistant Director Kathleen Wishart

71

3rd Assistant Director Jodi Moore
Floor Runner Katie McCorkindale
Driver Patrick Harkins Snr
Script Supervisor Dorothy Connolley
Focus Puller Alan McSheehy
Steadicam Operator Simon Bray
Clapper Loader Neil Davidson
Key Grip Terry Pate
Additional Grip Iain Johnstone
Crane Operator Graham Wright
Jimmy Jib Kent Wilson
Video Operator Colette Valvona
Riggers Billy Wilson, John Butler
Sound Recordist Brian Howell
Boom Operators Alan MacNicol, Tony Cook
Lighting Gaffer Stuart Farmer
Lighting Technicians Paul Bates, Derek Guyer,
  Frank McConalogue, Graham Walker
Make-up Designer Sarah Fidelo
Make-up Assistant Marie Rodgers
Make-up Daily Karen Campbell
Assistant Costume Designer Ruth Kirton
Wardrobe Assistant Louise Borland
Art Director Jean Kerr
Production Buyer Penny Crawford
Assistant Art Director Niki Longmuir
Standby Art Directors Ewen Duncan, Irene Harris
Art Department Assistants Alan Payne, Elaine Robertson
Storyboard Artist Rob McCallum
Graffiti Artist Tommy Keenan
Scenic Artist Kelvin Guy
Property Master Chris Cull
Chargehand Dressing Propman Paul McNamara
Dressing Props David Miller
Standby Props Ann McCredie

Standby Carpenters Paul Murphy, Peter Knotts
Construction Manager Jamie Baxter
Construction Crew Ben Barry, Don Clark
Carpenters Eric Harrison, Dennis Murphy
Master Painters Jim Patrick, Henry Gallagher
Painters Mark Kennedy, Carol Soutar, Stephen Bryce,
   Malcolm Rogan
Unit Caterers G.T. Caterers
Unit Nurse Stefania Swiatek

S&YPF Trainees
Production Trainees Becky Mark Lawson, Andrew Maxwell
Camera Trainees Paula McEwan, Hilary Foster

Baby Coco by Nik Williams of Animated Extras
Puppeteers Geoff Felix, Colin Purves, Rik Marr,
   Tracy O'Brien, Sue Howard, Jonathan Klahr
Stunt Performer Michael Scott-Law

Granton Star Cause Production
Production Manager Fiona Henderson
1st Assistant Director Ian Madden
2nd Assistant Director Alison Goring
3rd Assistant Director Ted Mitchell
Script Supervisor Janis Watt
Focus Puller Alan McSheehy
Steadicam Operators Howard Smith, Al Rae
Clapper Loader Alick Fraser
Fly Photography Rod Clarke
Fly Wrangler Rupert Barrington
Key Grip Jamie Coulter
Additional Grip Terry Pate
Sound Recordist Alan Brereton
Boom Operator Becky Thomson

Lighting Gaffer Alex Mackenzie
Lighting Technicians Mick Toher, Frank McConalogue
Make-up Designer Marilyn MacDonald
Make-up Assistant Nikki Brannan
Wardrobe Supervisor Fiona King
Art Director Rohan Banyard
Assistant Art Director Cliondha Harkin
Property Master Tony Sheridan
Standby Props Paul McNamara
Standby Carpenter Andy Duly
Unit Drivers Chris Dooks, Ashley Johnstone

SB&FT Trainees
Costume Trainee Cat Shirley
AD Tim Bain
Production Karen Wood
SYPF Trainee Cathy Delves
Unit Stills Renzo Mazzolini, Bill Stephenson

Post Production
Sound Designer Andrew Hulme
Dubbing Editor John Gow
Dubbing Mixers Douglas S. Murray, Mark Berger
Assistant Sound Editor Gerard Roche
Dubbing Facilities Ardmore Sound, Ireland
Digital Visual Effects by The Film Factory at VTR
Visual Effects Supervisor/Producer Simon Giles
Visual Effects Compositors Sally Clayton, Peter Connelly
Visual Effects Animator Steve Begg
Film Recording Zoe Cain, Trevor Young
Post Production Facilities First Cut
Film Negative Cutting Mike Fraser
Opticals and Titles General Screen Enterprises
Optical Liaison Graham Hoddell

74

Post Production Consultant Mark Gravil
Grader Colin Coull
Original Processing by Technicolor
Prints by Metrocolor
Titles Directors Luke Pendrell at antirom, Dylan Kendle at Pink
Flame Artist Tom Sparks at Smoke and Mirrors
Camera Equipment supplied by GHS Motion Picture Services
Lighting Equipment supplied by Lee Lighting
Legal Services Andrew J. Curtis at Russells

The Producers would like to thank:
The Edinburgh Development Fund
Eddie Dick
Colin Pons
Silverknowes Primary School
DLC, Glasgow
West Pilton Neighbourhood Centre
Jonathan Sissons
DJ Sheik & DJ Silencer on decks
Nick Dean on trumpet
Everyone at Wark Clements

In memoriam

Simon Dodd & Alex McKenzie

Archive
Time Lapse Photography Simon Kerwin Carroll
Marina Productions, France, supplied the MrMen/Little Miss Animation. C. Marina Productions/Mister Films Ltd/France 3 1997.
Womb footage from World of the Unborn, courtesy of Channel 4 Television.
Go Go Archipelago courtesy of Umbrella Productions.

Music

Insect Royalty
Performed by Primal Scream
Words & Music by Primal Scream
Published by EMI Music Publishing Ltd / Complete /
Copyright Control Courtesy of Creation Records / SINE

Maracana Madness
Performed by E-Klektic
Words & Music by E-Klektic
Published by Wall of Sound
Courtesy of Wall of Sound Recordings

Break
Performed by The Gyres
Words & Music by McLinden / Lyons / McLinden
Published by BMG Music Publishing Ltd
Courtesy of Sugar Records

By The Time I Get To Phoenix
Performed by Glen Campbell
Words & Music by Jimmy Webb
Published by EMI Songs Ltd / Sony / ATV Music
Publishing
Courtesy of EMI Records Ltd

Nothing to be Done
Performed by The Pastels
Words & Music by Pastel, Wright, Taylor, Hayward,
Simpson
Published by Momentum Music Ltd
Courtesy of Fire Records

The Sweetest Embrace
Performed by Nick Cave & Barry Adamson
Words & Music by Cave / Adamson
Published by Mute Song
Courtesy of Mute Records

Stupid Thing
Performed by Paul Quinn & The Independent Group
Words & Music by Quinn / Horne / Kirk / Hodgens
Published by Postcard Publishing / Polygram Music
Publishing Ltd
Courtesy of Postcard Records

Carbon
Performed by O Yuki Conjugate
Words & Music by Horberry / Hulme / McGeorge /
Mudford / Tétaz / Woodhead
Published by Copyright Control

Summer Wind
Performed by Jack L.
Words & Music by Mayrer / Mercer / Bradtke
Published by Editions Primus Rolf Budde KG / Warner
Bros Inc / Warner / Chappell Music Ltd
Courtesy of 38 S.C.R.

The Man with the Golden Arm
Performed by Barry Adamson
Words & Music by Adamson
Published by Mute Song
Courtesy of Mute Records

This is Carboottechnodisco
Performed by Bentley Rhythm Ace
Words & Music by March / Stokes
Published by Island Music Ltd
Courtesy of Parlophone Records

The Vibes Ain't Nothing But the Vibes
Performed by Barry Adamson
Words & Music by Adamson
Published by Mute Song
Courtesy of Mute Records

By the Time I get to Phoenix
Performed by Nick Cave
Words & Music by Jimmy Webb
Published by EMI Songs Ltd / Sony / ATVMusic
Publishing
Courtesy of Mute Records

That's Life
Performed by William 'Giggs' McGuigan
Words & Music by Kay / Gordon
Published by Polygram Music Publishing Ltd
Courtesy of Pioneer LDCE Ltd

Rhinestone Cowboy
Performed by Glenn Campbell
Words & Music by Larry Weiss
Published by Warner / Chappell Music Ltd
Courtesy of EMI Records Ltd

Wonderwall
Performed by The Nat Sanderson Sound
Words & Music by Noel Gallagher
Published by Oasis Music / Creation Songs Ltd / Sony /
ATV Music Publishing Ltd
Courtesy of Creation Records / SINE

Ill Behaviour
Performed by The Soul Renegades
Words & Music by Smith / Henrickse
Published by Copyright Control
Courtesy of In Demand Recordings

Precious Maybe
Performed by Beth Orton
Words & Music by Beth Orton
Published by EMI Music Publishing
Courtesy of Heavenly Recordings / Deconstruction Ltd

Hot Love
Performed by Marc Bolan
Words & Music by Marc Bolan
Published by Onward Music Ltd
Courtesy of Straight Ahead Productions Ltd

Slow Graffiti
Performed by Belle & Sebastian
Words & Music by Belle & Sebastian
Published by Copyright Control
Courtesy of Jeepster Records

Demonoid
Performed by Technoanimal
Words & Music by Flesh / Mart
Published by Copyright Control
Courtesy of City Slang Records

I Still Miss You
Performed by Arab Strap
Words & Music by Arab Strap
Published by Copyright Control
Courtesy of Chemikal Underground Records

Going Nowhere
Performed by Oasis
Words & Music by Noel Gallagher
Published by Oasis Music / Creation Songs Ltd / Sony /
ATV Music Publishing Ltd
Courtesy of Creation Records / SINE

Nautical Dub
Performed by Porter Ricks
Words & Music by Mellweg & Koner
Published by BMG / UFA Musikverlage
Courtesy of Basic Channel

79

The Cantino Sessions
Performed by Death in Vegas
Words & Music by Fearless / Hellier
Published by Deconstruction Songs Ltd / BMG Publishing
UK Ltd
Courtesy of Deconstruction Ltd

Claiming Marilyn
Performed by Death in Vegas
Words & Music by Fearless / Hellier
Published by Deconstruction Songs Ltd / BMG Publishing
UK Ltd
Courtesy of Deconstruction Ltd

Re-arranged Face / Someplace South of Here
Performed by A Small Good Thing
Words & Music by Fazzini / Hulme / Sedgwick
Published by Copyright Control
Courtesy of Soleilmoon Recordings

Leave Home
Performed by The Chemical Brothers
Words & Music by Simons / Rowlands / Baxter
Published by MCA Music Ltd / BMG Music Publishing
Courtesy of Virgin Records Ltd

Shag
Performed by The Sons of Silence
Music by Mudford
Published by Mudford

Toujours L'Amour
Performed by Dimitri from Paris
Words & Music by Dimitri from Paris
Published by Blonde Music
Courtesy of Disorient Records

Moving Heart Source / 40 Watt Ovals
80

Performed by A Small Good Thing
Words & Music by Fazzini / Hulme / Sedgwick
Published by Copyright Control
Courtesy of The Leaf Label

Bobby Dazzler
Performed by The Sons of Silence
Words & Music by Mudford / Gardiner / Hulme
Published by Copyright Control
Courtesy of The Leaf Label

On Your Own
Performed by The Verve
Words & Music by Jones / Salisbury / McCabe / Ashcroft
Published by EMI Virgin Music Publishing Ltd
Courtesy of Virgin Records Ltd

Soundtrack Album released by
EMI Records
Screenplay published by
Methuen Books
Dolby in selected theatres
Filmed on location in Edinburgh & Glasgow
A Picture Palace North / Umbrella Productions Film for
Channel 4 in association with the Yorkshire Media
Production Agency
Part funded by the European Regional Development Fund
The Scottish Arts Council National Lottery Fund
The Glasgow Film Fund
All characters and events in this motion picture are
fictitious. Any similarity to actual events or persons, living
or dead, is purely coincidental and unintentional.
© Channel 4 Television Corporation MCMXCVIII

METHUEN SCREENPLAYS

☐ BEAUTIFUL THING	Jonathan Harvey	£6.99
☐ THE ENGLISH PATIENT	Anthony Minghella	£7.99
☐ THE CRUCIBLE	Arthur Miller	£6.99
☐ THE WIND IN THE WILLOWS	Terry Jones	£7.99
☐ PERSUASION	Jane Austen, adapted by Nick Dear	£6.99
☐ TWELFTH NIGHT	Shakespeare, adapted by Trevor Nunn	£7.99
☐ THE KRAYS	Philip Ridley	£7.99
☐ THE AMERICAN DREAMS (THE REFLECTING SKIN & THE PASSION OF DARKLY NOON)	Philip Ridley	£8.99
☐ MRS BROWN	Jeremy Brock	£7.99
☐ THE GAMBLER	Dostoyevsky, adapted by Nick Dear	£7.99
☐ TROJAN EDDIE	Billy Roche	£7.99
☐ THE WINGS OF THE DOVE	Hossein Amini	£7.99
☐ THE ACID HOUSE TRILOGY	Irvine Welsh	£8.99
☐ THE LONG GOOD FRIDAY	Barrie Keeffe	£6.99
☐ SLING BLADE	Billy Bob Thornton	£7.99

• All Methuen Drama books are available through mail order or from your local bookshop.

Please send cheque/eurocheque/postal order (sterling only) Access, Visa, Mastercard, Diners Card, Switch or Amex.

☐☐☐☐☐☐☐☐☐☐☐☐☐☐☐☐

Expiry Date: _____ Signature: _____

Please allow 75 pence per book for post and packing U.K.
Overseas customers please allow £1.00 per copy for post and packing.

ALL ORDERS TO:

Methuen Books, Books by Post, TBS Limited, The Book Service, Colchester Road, Frating Green, Colchester, Essex CO7 7DW.

NAME: _____

ADDRESS: _____

_____

Please allow 28 days for delivery. Please tick box if you do not
wish to receive any additional information ☐

Prices and availability subject to change without notice.